Being a Christian When the Chips Are Down

HELMUT THIELICKE

Being a Christian When the Chips Are Down

Translated by

H. GEORGE ANDERSON

FORTRESS PRESS PHILADELPHIA

Translated by H. George Anderson from the German *Der Christ im Ernstfall* ©Verlag Herder Freiburg im Breisgau 1977.

Published in Great Britain under the title *Facing Life's Questions* by William Collins Sons & Co., Ltd., 1979.

Library of Congress Cataloging in Publication Data

Thielicke, Helmut, 1908-
Being a Christian when the chips are down.

Translation of Der Christ im Ernstfall.
1. Christian life—Lutheran authors. 2. Church year—Meditations. I. Title.
BV4503.T5213 248'.48'41 78-54562
ISBN 0-8006-0541-1

7411K78 Printed in the United States of America 1-541

To The Benedictine Abbey
St. Gabriel in der Steiermark
in friendship

Contents

PART I

Basic Questions

1 *Who Am I?*

I once found myself in the company of some car owners, each of whom sang the praises of his own automobile. One said, "I have a car that can cruise effortlessly at 85 on the interstate." The other said, "You should have seen the way mine handled Pikes Peak! No vapor lock or overheating, whereas the luxury cars had to pull over and cool off!" A girl who knows she has an attractive figure and enjoys flirting could not be more conceited than these men were. They acted precisely as if those cars of theirs had become *themselves* and therefore they had been bragging about themselves.

Another experience of the same sort happened when I told a student, "You are a quite gifted young man." He blushed at that, as though I had praised him. I then said to him, "You don't need to blush, because it wasn't at all my intention to call you a fine fellow or a great guy. I merely said that you have been granted *gifts* which were not of your own making. They have really been 'bestowed' on you. So *you* don't need to blush!"

Both of these stories are very significant, because something important shows up in them. Human beings have a most remarkable inclination to identify with anything that adds to their prestige or lifts their social standing, be it an automobile, a powerful position in business or politics, or their intellectual abilities. They latch on to these things and identify with them to the point of saying, "This is who I am."

On the other hand I could recount cases where exactly the opposite happened—where someone said, "That's *not* me." There is the defendant who is being tried for murder. He and his attorney take great pains to show that the *environment* in which he grew up, his disadvantaged home, and his ill-fated development fostered criminal tendencies—in fact caused them in the first place. Thus, to a certain extent, he is to be "excused."

And one further scene: Perhaps I awake some morning, and I am upset over a dream I have had. In the dream I have done something so dreadful that I would be locked up because of it. Instinctively I ask myself, "Is there really such a rapist and murderer, such a hateful schemer, hiding in me?" But in the next moment I tell myself, "That's certainly not you. That is the id, the subconscious in you; but these depths of your heart are covered by the lily-white vest of an upstanding citizen."

One could cite Adam and Eve as scene number three. It was exactly the same way with them. When they both had eaten the forbidden fruit and God confronted them with their disobedience, Adam said, "The woman you gave me handed me the apple." And Eve said, "The serpent did it." Thus each of them was saying, "I am not to be identified with my deed. I am only the result and product of forces *outside* myself over which I have no control."

We can summarize the essence of these observations as follows: I identify myself with everything that is great and fine and positive in my life. Then I say, "That's who I am," whether it's a matter of talents, a powerful motor, or a bank account. And conversely, I disassociate myself from everything that puts me in the wrong or that is shocking or questionable in my life. Then I say, "That's *not* me."

Now one of the surprising twists about being a Christian is that we must totally revise our attitudes on these two points. The Sermon on the Mount, for example, sees through our white respectable vests. It doesn't say, "Of course, my good man, you are your vest." It says, "You are what is beneath that vest." And what's the problem *there*? Let me cite an example. In the Sermon on the Mount Jesus Christ gives an exposition of the ancient commandment "Thou shalt not kill." Now probably none of us is a murderer, so we can calmly tune him out. But Jesus continues, "It's not only stabbing someone that makes you a murderer. If you 'merely' hate your brother, you are a murderer." That means that we have the inclination to murder within us; that we have, so to speak, gone through the first stages of the act of murder, and that it is these thoughts of ours, or more precisely, of mine, that make me a murderer. Even a poet like Adalbert Stifter (in whose work only nice people and a neat world seem appropriate) has said exactly the same thing: Every one of us has a tiger within, and we never know to what lengths we might go if some nervous disorder robbed us of the inhibitions of our normal and conscious life.

Such talk might seem harsh and downright destructive. One might well ask, "How could anyone live with an outlook like that?" And yet he who preached the Sermon on the Mount intended for it to comfort us and to give us a totally new lease on life.

Specifically, when he confronts us about what lies behind our white vests, about that spot within us where we are potential murderers or adulterers, he wants to tell us, "Look, I do know how things are with you. I came down here from the command post of heaven to be with you in the grubbiest trenches on the front lines as you fight your inevitable battles with others and with yourselves. Indeed I know how it is. I have suffered there myself. Ultimately I had to hold out against three demonic temptations; I have stood on your battlefield. My heart, too, beat faster. But now I must tell you something," Christ continues. "In my father's house in heaven there are no cloakrooms where white vests are checked in as passports to heaven; there are tables festively set where I dine with my earthly friends. Every one of these guests is a very dubious type, just like you. But that is precisely the good news: you may come exactly as you *are* and may expect to be received. You have no further need for the camouflage of a white vest. You are loved and welcomed just as you are, even behind your vest. For you come as my brothers and sisters. I am bringing you with me, even though it wasn't at all easy to 'awaken' you, to pry you away, and to bring you here."

Next we need to rethink matters in the opposite direction. I cited examples of car owners and a talented student which showed how we human beings are inclined to identify ourselves with everything that is positive and enhancing to our lives. That *also* changes when we become Christian, for then we learn to be thankful for everything good and great in our lives. And if we are thankful, then we are really saying, "I am not that; I have received it as a gift."

I had that experience during the air raids. Before when I went into my book-lined study, I would say to myself, "All of this is your learning and skill; it belongs to you; it is, in a manner of speaking, an extension of your ego." But then, when the bombs began to fall and houses all around caved in, I reminded myself, "It is really not so self-evident that all this belongs to you; it all can be taken away; it is only given to you as a trust." For that reason I began to be thankful for every day that I was allowed to keep those treasures of mine.

The same thing holds true for us in other matters. Anything that we have, our family, our friends, our health, the sight of sea and mountains, is no longer so obviously "ours," once we learn to thank God for it. It becomes, instead, an undeserved gift. That gives a new and joyful vitality to our life. At the same time we learn to live with greater awareness. In every moment we realize anew that we are led by loving hands and blessed by a fatherly heart. We no longer plod dully along; we suddenly discover what "living" really means. We live in the name of miracle, and this miracle is that we are gifted human beings; we have a home in this world and in the world to come. We don't need to fool ourselves and others any more. We may come as we are. Life is worth living, because it has meaning. Those who have learned to give thanks have been liberated to live.

How I Know Myself and How God Knows Me

Recently I was talking to someone. He was about sixty and wore an elegant tailored suit. In fact everything about him was well-groomed and, one might say, perfect. He told me, "*Once* in my life I made a wrong move. I should have been a musician, and then I would have made something of myself. Instead, I had to take over my father's business. Basically, though, I was no businessman. I have spent my whole life on something that actually is foreign to me. So my life ended up as a heap of ashes before it had ever really caught fire."

I responded, "Aren't you too pessimistic? Why are you feeling so sorry for youself? You have, in fact, gotten somewhere in life."

He: "Gotten 'somewhere'? Sure. To a big house and a fine car—which may have caught your eye when you came in. Of course, in a way you are right. I have certainly gotten somewhere. But I have not found *myself*—that's the worst of it."

I: "What do you mean by that?"

He answered very carefully (and one had the impression that he had thought long and hard about the question), "Well, I believe that every person has a unique vocation. We are designed, so to speak, for a specific life plan. This design for our life, however, is only a bare outline."

Then I interrupted him with what may have been a somewhat frivolous remark, but I wanted to use this conversation about his life to draw him a little further out of his shell.

I asked him, "You said that everyone carries this design for his life around with him, but only in outline form. Have you ever seen one of these outlines?"

He looked at me somewhat reproachfully, as though I had made light of a matter that he took very seriously.

"No," he replied, "obviously I have *not* seen one of these outlines. Haven't you gotten my point? You don't see these things, you *feel* them. *That's* why you're here. *That's* what you must be. You are designed for *that*—and I was certainly destined for music. But you see, I never filled in the outline of my design. I just spattered a few drops of paint around it. Viewed from a higher perspective my life is a sorry sight."

Then I said, "If I understand you correctly, you reproach yourself by saying, 'I cannot identify with the person I have become. I haven't found my true identity.'"

He replied like a shot, "That's exactly the word I've been looking for. I can't identify with the person I've become."

I will conclude my little report on our conversation at this point; obviously it went on much longer. Why have I recounted it?

Well, I believe that this question, "What am I?"—this question about our identity—occupies every one of us. When we are young we ask, "What shall I become?" Frequently this question is not only (thank heaven!) meant to ask "How can I earn the most money?" but *also* to ask, "Why am I here? How can I best spend my life? How can I best become 'myself'? How can I not only 'get somewhere,' but 'come to myself'?"

It is amazing how these questions have continued to fascinate the minds of philosophers and poets. They are among the favorite themes of Max Frisch and stand at the heart of his novel *My Name Is to Be Gantenbein.* Karl Marx claimed that human beings were what their social and economic relationships made them. Sartre, on the other hand, thought that persons became "fixed" by their surroundings, which expected them to fulfill a certain role; they must be "just so," and for that reason they are hindered by this social pressure from becoming themselves, or coming to themselves.

Most readers are probably not very interested in how this theme of identity—this question of "Who is the real me"—is treated in *literature.* They would rather know if and when this question occurs in their own lives. I would like to say a little more on that point.

At some time in your life you have certainly received the impression that the picture your colleagues, perhaps, or good friends have of you varies considerably from the one you have of yourself. Sometimes when you reach out to shake hands with a competitor in sports or in business, others are impressed by this gesture and think, "He *does* have a noble attitude; what a gentleman." You yourself know, however, that you heartily wish he would go to blazes, but that you are clever enough to conceal it. Of course it can also happen the other way around. You have intended something to be kind and selfless, but others attribute it to egotistical motives. In both cases you ask yourself "Which is the real *me*? Am I what others see in me, or what I myself see?"

I would like to cite two examples that could lead to the performing of a couple of mental experiments with this identity question.

Example number one: You have watched a detective show on television. The criminals who appear in it usually evoke a certain stereotyped image for us. They are filled with greed or thirst for revenge (that's why they murder people); but outwardly they are genteel and have a remarkable talent for masking their real character. (That is precisely the intriguing part about detective shows—one always picks the wrong suspect.) But in reality is this shadowy character *only* greedy or vengeful? Doesn't his soul have still other regions unexplored by the film—in fact unreachable by the camera's eye? Isn't it possible that this hardened criminal now and then feels a trace of pity for an oppressed fellow human being and then is able to help that person selflessly? Couldn't he now and then love honorably and even act honorably? Which side of the crook is the real one? Again the images diverge from one another.

Example number two: I was once on hand when a young man who had gotten into many scrapes and had nearly broken his mother's heart (he had even been in prison once) sat down at the piano and played a chorale from the "St. Matthew Passion." He played it like a prayer, full of emotion and involvement. It touched me deeply. Then his sister whispered in my ear "That hypocrite!"

Was he *really* a hypocrite? What was his true and basic nature? Was he in his inmost self the one who always had his hand in someone else's pocket in order to indulge in an apparently evil and easy life? Or was he in his inmost self the one who played that chorale, crying out for deliverance in it, despising himself and trying to wash the filth out of his soul?

None of us can judge who he *truly* was; perhaps he never even knew himself. Perhaps God alone knows. Perhaps God has said to himself, "This man hungered and thirsted after righteousness, and he despised himself. Therefore he is dearer to me—despite the shady areas of his life—than many self-assured and self-righteous people in all their immaculate integrity."

In the final days of the Second World War Pastor Dietrich Bonhoeffer was hanged by the Gestapo. He had to die because his faith had compelled him to take a confessional stand against the Nazi regime. His guards and fellow prisoners held him in high regard, because he never let himself give in, and because even in chains he remained his own master. To be sure, he also knew times of discouragement. Yet he kept those times hidden from others. Some poems from the period of his imprisonment have been preserved, and one of them deals with this question of "Who am I." It even has that title. I want to quote a few lines from it for you:

> Who am I? They often tell me
> I would step from my cell's confinement
> calmly, cheerfully, firmly,
> like a squire from his country-house. . . .
>
> Am I then really all that which other men tell of?
> Or am I only what I know of myself,
> restless and longing and sick, like a bird in a cage, . . .
> weary and empty at praying, at thinking, at making, . . .
>
> Who am I? This or the other? . . .
> Am I both at once? A hypocrite before others,
> and before myself a contemptibly woebegone weakling? . . .
> Who am I? They mock me, these lonely questions of mine,
> Whoever I am, thou knowest, O God, I am thine.

What does it signify to say that God knows me and that I am his? It means *first* that we human beings neither understand ourselves nor our fellowmen completely. We know neither our own identity nor that of others. But that need not trouble us. Our image is held in the heart of God. He knows all there is to know about us.

And that leads to a second point: The thought that God knows all there is to know about us could also be somewhat frightening. To be seen through by someone to the farthest corner of our soul, to be "x-rayed" through and through, is a frightful thought.

Yet if what Jesus has told us about his Father is true, then it is not frightful; it is at once beautiful and comforting to be "seen through" in such a way. For we know that he understands us in love and seeks us amid pain.

Goethe once said that we can only understand that which we love. In God's heart we are loved infinitely. Therefore we are also understood infinitely. We are understood by someone who is sympathetic to us.

If it were possible for a *human being* to see through us so completely it would be frightening. Our fears would drive us to decide, "I'd better not show my face around here again." Bonhoeffer, however, said, "Whoever I am, thou knowest, O God, I am thine." There is One who declares that he is on my side, whoever I am.

2 *No Religious Questions Any More?*

A 29-year-old engineer wrote me, "It used to be that people had religious questions. They asked about the salvation of their souls. They were interested in life after death and a continuing existence in the beyond. But isn't that sort of thing far behind us today? The most we ever ask about is the meaning of our life, and only our earthly life at that! We ask less about God than about the possibility of a human community. Isn't that the reason why so many people disassociate themselves from the church today?"

I tried to answer him as follows: You are right. Our chief question is indeed the inquiry after the meaning of life. But what is that? I read an obituary for an engineer that bore the title "A Life Given to Air Conditioning." Perhaps you've seen a picture in some magazine of a skyscraper with sheer glass walls and, hanging on that vast surface, the tiny, lonely figure of a window washer. By the time he finally completes his Sisyphean task and reaches the ground, the upper stories are already dirty and the whole process starts over again. Can anyone give one's life to air conditioning or window washing? Is that the *meaning* of someone's life? What happens to me then when I have to retire? Then I no longer perform any purposeful activities. What is left of me then? Why am I still around?

It is particularly among capable and active people who retire and suddenly sense that they are useless and forgotten that I repeatedly find feelings of despair. They have seen the meaning of their life as lying exclusively in their vocational skills. When these skills are no longer needed, everything becomes meaningless. A vast emptiness yawns before them.

When I speak of "meaning" I obviously intend more than simply the purpose which I serve by my activity. "Meaning" implies the reason for my existence, in which I can be involved and for which it is worth living. (Air conditioning or window washing, however, don't qualify.) This line of questioning goes far beyond my own life. I am asking about someone who has given me life and who has given it to me "for something"; for example, to love humanity, to help other people, and to be there when they need me. If I am conscious that this "someone"—we Christians would substitute "God"—has given me my life, that he watches over me and accompanies me, then my life has value in his eyes even when I am old or an invalid. When I can no longer fulfill any purpose or perform any useful function, my life still is not meaningless on that account. For I know that I am and remain bound up with that "someone," and that he will remain true to me even through death. The question about meaning, therefore, has something to do with the question about God after all—even something to do with Easter and the victory over death.

Furthermore, it seems to me that exactly the same thing is true of your second question, the one about human community. Why was it that the "rock generation" became in our minds a symbol for social conflict, a sort of antitype to human community? Frequently they grew up in homes where they were unwelcome. They felt themselves pushed around, and therefore not "accepted." What was thus planted in them as seeds of hostility and rejection they later reacted against through aggression. We can, of course, only love other people and be available to them when we accept them (even if they sometimes don't fit our particular mold). We are only able to accept them, however, when we ourselves—in contrast to the rock generation—are accepted. One could reduce the whole gospel to the simple formula that God has thus accepted us and that he wants to be there when we need him. Once we are aware that our life is grounded in the miracle of acceptance by a figure like Jesus we experience the fascinating freedom ourselves of being there when we're needed and of being able to accept others.

Concluding question: Have you therefore, in this letter, really formulated an *alternative* to religious questions (as was obviously your intention)? Or could it be that you have only transformed the old questions in such a way that they face you in a new form? They are clearly indestructible and remain ever fresh. We must only see to it that we are alert enough to discover them.

3 *Why Be Afraid of Life?*

Some time ago a number of questions, similar to the famous Gallup poll, was posed to a group of predominantly young people, mostly of college age. One of these questions read: "What is the basic feeling you have about life?" Sixty percent answered with staggering straightforwardness: "Fear." How does it happen that people who give no impression of being fearful or cowed give a strange answer like that?

Anxiety About Life

If one wishes to ascertain whether a person is fearful—or perhaps "anxious" would be better—one would be inclined to explore that person's attitude toward life's dangers, particularly toward death. Any attempt to check the accuracy of that survey in this way would very quickly reach a dead end. For it cannot be said of our generation that it is especially anxious about death. People have occasionally noted with surprise that fearlessness in the face of death by no means requires any sort of "religious support," but that religiously indifferent, even atheistic and nihilistic persons can possess a decidedly cold-blooded attitude toward death.

One would not be far from the truth in seeing the answer to that survey as an expression of fear of life, rather than fear of death. It was fear of guilt before the divine judge that filled the medieval monk Luther and wrung from him the question, "How can I find a gracious God?" Today it is fear of the future that shakes people, anxiety of the immense and unplumbed possibilities that life conceals. Where once stood God the judge, there is now a vacuum, an empty spot.

Perhaps Christian proclamation should take that change quite seriously and seek out people who are plagued with anxiety at the brink of that abyss, or in it. In fact the Holy Book of Christianity again and again addresses humanity not only about its sin, but even more about its fear. And few sentences are repeated as often as the call to God's peace which is customarily introduced with the words "Fear not."

In order to understand the essence of this anxiety it would be well to consider the linguistic roots of the word itself. "Anxiety" comes from the Latin word "angustiae," signifying lack of breathing space, suffocation, which can appear in extreme cases of anxiety as *angina pectoris.* It is characteristic of the term "anxiety" that it denotes a condition in which the cause of my anxiety fades into the background or does not even appear. This feeling of being threatened by something indefinable is the essence of anxiety.

In order to understand that feeling, one might think of the image of the Midgard serpent in Germanic mythology: Beyond the horizon, the great serpent rings the earth, so that we are ensnared in those great coils. The whole world is surrounded by the sinister. It weighs over everything, even the fun and festivity that humanity might celebrate in this world which is locked in such a fearful embrace. At this point the whole terror of anxiety comes to light. As long as I am simply afraid, that is, as long as I fear something definite, I continue to have hope as well. I fear I have cancer, but maybe it is only a harmless swelling, or maybe there is an unexpected possibility of cure. I fear that my missing son is dead, but perhaps he is still alive.

Under the anxious curse of the Midgard serpent, however, everything is different. Here the world in its totality, together with all things frightening and hopeful, is placed in question.

The divinities to whom humanity flees, including the powers of hope, are overshadowed by the twilight of the gods. In times of great catastrophe the serpent, so to speak, draws its coils tighter.

Dubious Ways of Dealing with Anxiety

It would be surprising if humanity didn't do everything possible to free itself from this anxiety. Ernst Jüngers's essay "The Man in the Moon" is an impressive description of how people make the attempt. "When it comes to meaning—that is, when it comes to a recognizable order in history—my existence is more hopeless (and therefore more anxiety-ridden) than any earthly one. I—as a man on the moon—can't locate my bearings. (I find myself in an icy, cratered moonscape.) Since I have given up brooding about the meaning of my life, I find that I get along pretty well." Thus people try to deal with anxiety, not by seeking to find meaning in spite of it all, as Faust did, but by ignoring the question of meaning, living a happy-go-lucky existence, practically vegetating.

A striking example of this way of handling the question of meaning—and therefore anxiety—is the fate of the famous Englishman, Lawrence of Arabia, who became world-renowned through his role as leader of the Arab revolt during the First World War. Churchill said of him that he was one of the greatest hopes of the British Empire. After his brilliant wartime activities in the desert, the world-famous colonel enlisted as a common soldier in the ground personnel of the Royal Air Force. Why? "I do it in order to serve a mechanical purpose, not as a leader, but as the shadow of a machine . . . It is a blessing to be only a part of a machine. You learn that it doesn't depend entirely on you." Lawrence had accomplished great things. He had assumed great responsibility for the Arabs who idolized him. In the end, however, his efforts on their behalf came to nothing, and the meaninglessness of everything he had accomplished crashed in upon him. In that moment the fear of life conquered this bravest of men. And so he tried to escape by dehumanizing himself to the point of wanting to be nothing more than a tiny screw in a great machine.

This approach saves us from fear of life and from meaninglessness, not by repeatedly raising the questions of meaning and structure, but by not raising them at all, by thus ceasing to be human, by becoming anonymous, fading into the crowd, or by becoming merely the instrumentality for processes and functions whose purpose and goal no longer concern us. We could find peace in that way. It is the deceptive peace of a technical nirvana, the peace of self-surrender, the flight into detail and superficiality. This alternative confronts us with overwhelming force in current life-styles. There are few things in contemporary life that do not bear this sign of fear and flight from life on their foreheads.

The Conquest of Anxiety

Having said that, we face the question of whether, instead of those deceptive "detours," there can be a *true* conquest of this anxiety.

The Christian cannot speak of such a conquest without meditating on him who said of himself, "In the world you have tribulation, but be of good cheer, I have overcome the world" (John 16:33). The surprising thing about the biblical message is this: you see the opposite to fear and anxiety in *love.* "There is no fear (one could just as well say "anxiety") in love" (1 John 4:18).

That is surprising because (in contrast to what one would expect) bravery, heroism, and a stiff upper lip are not pitted against anxiety in this passage. All of those ways would suppress anxiety, not conquer it. The *positive* power which conquers anxiety is love. We can understand what that means only when we have grasped the deepest sources of anxiety—

when we learn that anxiety is a destroyed bond and that love is the bond restored. Because of Jesus, one realizes that there is a fatherly basis for this world and that one is beloved; then one loses one's anxiety. One does not lose it because the threatening powers no longer exist. In Dürer's picture "Knight, Death and the Devil" the evil forces still lurk along the path, but they no longer have power over the knight. Put in figurative language, one could say, "If my Father gives me his hand, if I am aware of this hand, then even in the darkest forest I am no longer afraid."

If someone is anxious and knows about Christ, then one can start out by being certain of this: I am not alone with my anxiety; he has *also* endured it. In that way an entirely new relationship to the future comes into being. It is no longer the fog-shrouded landscape where I anxiously keep watch because somewhere out there dark dangers are brewing against me. No, everything is entirely different. We do not know what is coming, but we know *who* is coming. The final hour belongs to us. We need have no fear of the next minute.

4 *Does Our Life Have Any Meaning?*

I know of no better illustration of the question concerning meaning in our life than Jesus' parable about the prodigal son (Luke 15). In order to make that clear, though, one must avoid interpreting this parable in a moralistic way—as though it concerned a wayward boy who ran away from home, to the foreign legion so to speak, or at least to a foreign land, where he went completely to ruin and at the last moment snatched himself from disaster. This story has a meaning totally different from that of a simple moral tale. It has, as it were, *many* levels of meaning, so that one can hardly exhaust them. At this point I will bring out only *one* of these various levels.

Estrangement and a Strange Land

The story is about a young man who asks his father for his share of the inheritance so that he can go off to a strange land.

Why does he want to leave?

It doesn't have to be some vague lust for adventure that drives him to go. Would his father, in that case, have given him the money so willingly and let him leave without batting an eye?

Probably the young man leaves because he wants to find himself. Sometimes in order to find oneself one has to go one's own way. At home, under the parental roof, he had to do what his *father* wanted or what family custom required. He felt dependent there. He couldn't do what *he* wanted to do, but only what was expected of him. He was thus not his own man; he was "owned" by the customs and laws of his family. Especially since he was the younger brother, he just never had a chance to develop on his own.

Therefore he left home to find himself. One could even say that he left in order to learn what freedom was. And this freedom that enticed him and promised him that he could at last be "himself"—this freedom appeared to him to be freedom from all obligations.

At this point, however, the story takes a surprising turn. It tells us that the prodigal son squandered all he possessed on bad companions, loose women, and miscellaneous riffraff. He was finally reduced to begging, deserted by everyone; he ended up tending pigs and eating out of their trough.

Thus, although his departure may have had elements of idealism, and a certain intense longing for freedom may have driven him on, it wasn't long before he failed miserably. He sought freedom, but he soon found himself enslaved to his drives, his ambition, and the fear of loneliness, in comparison to which any companion, no matter how questionable, seemed preferable. He was enslaved to the Mammon with which he pandered to his passions. And *therefore* he was not free; he was obligated in a new way. This new obligation, however, was more terrible than the obligation he used to complain about at home.

What had happened? Simply this: that in contrast to what he had set out to do, instead of finding himself, he became lost (the German title for this parable is "The Lost Son"). In his search for selfhood, he thought he would find himself if he could just develop all his gifts and abilities. In fact he was able to develop in the "freedom" of a strange land. But what did his "personal style," his "own way" turn out to be? Was it his so-called "better self," was it his idealistic motives that came to expression? Maybe so, but in any case along with his self-fulfillment the *dark* sides of his nature also came to full flower: urges, ambition, fear, lust. To the degree that he developed himself, he also became enslaved to the dark forces within himself which showed up as part of his own development. So he ended up in the brutalizing misery of a hired hand. Suddenly he was the most menial servant of all.

Now comes the second surprising twist. As he sat there in his miserable slavery, he yearned for the freedom which he had enjoyed as a child in his father's house. At once he realized that it was *true* freedom. In fact, he realized something else. Freedom is not the absence of obligation (that had turned out to be slavery), but freedom is only a special form of obligation. I have freedom only as a child of my father. I have freedom only when I live in harmony with my origin, when I am (to speak without metaphor) at peace with God. And when the young man decides to return home, he makes no moral decision against the enticements of that foreign land, moaning and groaning in self-reproach as is customary in such decisions. For him it is a move filled with trembling joy and the radiance of hope.

After all that has been said, it should certainly be clear why I have labeled this story as an important contribution to the question about the meaning of life. For I gain this meaning only when I find the *fulfillment* of my life, when I become what I was meant to be. And exactly at that point the prodigal son again becomes relevant.

On all of those wild-goose chases which were supposed to help him find himself he was forced to recognize that he did *not* find himself precisely when he went seeking self-fulfillment. He only came to himself when he came back to his father. That is because human beings are not like seeds that need only to live in order to develop their potential. They do not carry it all within themselves in rudimentary form that merely needs time to grow. Human beings are children of God who only achieve their potential if they grow into a mature relationship with their Parent; they miss their chance if they seek to become isolated egos or soloists in the art of life.

The Golden Sky

Perhaps some people who read these lines have seen those Gothic paintings in which the human figures are placed before a background of golden sky. This background portrays the uniqueness of humankind: that it stands in a special relation to the glory of God. Today an artist would portray the uniqueness of a person by evoking that person's individual features, by painting an "expressive" face—of course, only in the event that the subject had one!—and by emphasizing what was "in" the person portrayed. That is precisely what the Gothic painters do *not* do. The faces are in no way individualized; gesture, pose, and drapery are highly stylized. Individual characteristics are, so to speak, ignored, or at least not emphasized. And if many art historians think that individuality had not yet been "discovered," they are not entirely wrong, but they are only addressing a symptom and not the peculiar cause for this way of depicting human beings. Individuality was not yet discovered *because* the essence of humanity was not sought in some personal self-fulfillment, but by seeing humanity in the context of the glory of God.

In that way those painters expressed their conviction that the secret and the meaning of human life does not lie in aptitudes and personal characteristics but, one might say, in "inter-personal" characteristics, that is, in our relation to God for whom and from whom we live.

I obtain the freedom to be myself only when I become free for God. And because this being free for God—this Father-child relationship—is given me in Jesus Christ, it is really true that "whom the Son makes free is free indeed"(paraphrase of John 8:36). For the truth that is dealt with here is not the correctness of some doctrinal statement; it is a fact of our life, the fact that our existence is bound to the Father. Only those who have found God have also found themselves.

Once that has happened, however, the concern about fulfilling and realizing all our unique and personal gifts takes care of itself, so that our individuality is not given short shrift. For when we live and breathe in the freedom of our Father's house, we are at peace; we become free in regard to ourselves, because nothing ever can separate us from that love which has enfolded us, and because we don't have to worry about ourselves any more or about the dark sides of our personalities. There is, indeed, Someone in whom we find security and who remains faithful to us; there is Someone to whom we may come as we are.

Life is successful for us only when we find *this* life. If we fail to find it, we miss the whole point of our existence. We might make a great name for ourselves in the world, we might lack nothing in external goods, and people might bow and scrape to us. Yet we will have failed to find the meaning of our life.

When the father embraced his returning son, the boy had not only found his way home. He had found himself once again.

5 *How Can We Get a Fresh Start?*

It is amazing to see what difficulties we often have in understanding even the simplest and best-known concepts in Christianity. What "forgiveness" means, for example, or "justification." They often seem—if we consider the matter at all—to be made out of some extraterrestrial meteor material which cannot be alloyed with the metal of our earthly speech. For if we ponder the meaning that words like "forgive" and "pardon" have assumed in our normal usage it turns out that their original Christian significance eludes all attempts at fusing it with the contemporary meaning. I offer only one example of this sort:

"To Know All Is to Pardon All"

It's a common expression. Taken to its logical extreme it would mean: if I were able to reconstruct exactly the psychologically conditioned chain of events that led to a robbery and murder, I could not be angry with the criminal, because I would know all the causes that led him to do it. To say that everything is thus understandable to me means that ultimately the crime does not involve a responsible decision between good and evil, but simply an inevitable chain of events beyond good and evil. The scientist observing a chemical process in his test tube should not perceive the play of molecules and atoms as a battle between good and evil. Neither should we apply certain ethical categories when we observe the play of forces between self and environment which finally leads, through a necessary chain of cause-and-effect, to a robbery and murder. "To know all" on this basis hardly allows one to continue "is to pardon all." Rather one must say, "To know all means that there is nothing left to pardon, because the terrible thing that has happened is simply a necessary natural process."

At this point it becomes clear how totally different the Christian faith's thinking is: God indeed understands everything. "O Lord, thou has searched me and known me," says Psalm 139 (v. 1). And further, "Thou discernest my thoughts from afar": and still further, "Even before a word is on my tongue . . . thou knowest it altogether."

The psalm, however, does not draw some conclusion like: "Therefore, Lord, you can't blame me when I am not the way I should be." On the contrary, it says, "It is frightening, it is downright devastating, to think that there is someone who sees right through me. I want to take the wings of the morning and escape this all-penetrating gaze. I want to use the morning star for a darkroom light; I want to wrap myself in clouds and darkness. But it won't work. The divine gaze still finds me, and the night I have summoned becomes as bright as day. I remain exposed to that consuming, all-knowing gaze of God. It is the end of me."

If we now go on to say that this all-knowing God is our Father and wants to receive us—not because, but in spite, of what he knows about us—that is precisely the sort of eventuality that we could not have predicted, because it is based on a miracle of the divine heart that dazzles our minds. The fact that we are pardoned and that we can have a fresh start, that we therefore have a second chance is absolutely *not* based on the all-knowing God tracing back the causes of our inadequacy. It is based on something happening within God. Pardon is ultimately traceable neither to God's ability to know all, nor to his ability to forget all. We are no more capable of wrapping ourselves in the mantle of darkness than

God is able to cover us with the mantle of forgetfulness. Rather, by seeing everything that we are not allowed to be, he forgives us. What can this mean?

People Without a Past

In his drama, "Traveller Without Luggage," Anouilh tells a story that can help us along, even if it is quite non-Christian.

A young soldier has received a head wound in battle that totally robs him of his memory. He no longer knows his name or where he comes from, and he doesn't even know who his family is. This case is publicized by radio and newspapers in order to urge any relatives of the injured man to make themselves known. After a number of such responses have come in, the young man is sent on an itinerary in order to meet the respondents and to see if his parents are among them. At first there are only negative results and disappointments; then suddenly a family cries out as if with one voice "That's him, our son, our brother!" While his family recognize him, he—the man without a memory—cannot remember them. He stands unconcerned and terribly alien among his own people. They try to jog his memory by reminding him of particularly vivid impressions from his youth. They take him, for example, to a stairway over which, in anger, he had once thrown a young playmate, breaking the child's neck and arms—a frightful childhood experience. He, however, remains unmoved; his memory fails him even here. Then a housemaid whom he had once treated badly takes him aside and tearfully asks him if he remembers anything about what he did to her. When his memory gives no help on this occasion, she gives him proof of his identity; she tells him about a birthmark he bears. By means of a mirror he ascertains that it is true, so he can no longer dodge the certainty of who he is. Formerly he was someone who lived only in the present and had a future to shape. Now, however, he suddenly had a past. To have an identity means to have a past. And to have a past means to have guilt; it means to have baggage to carry; it means to be locked in by that which I have behind me. This situation is common to us all. Every time we submit an application we include biographical material and reveal our past. It is taken for granted that a person is identified by what is behind him. (Indeed, that is the claim of released prisoners—that they are identified with their former deeds and therefore refused employment.) On the whole, we are so accustomed to the baggage of our past that we hardly notice it any more. In this dramatic experiment, however, we are shown how terrifying it is suddenly to have to take an unaccustomed look at this baggage. The young man simply cannot bear it and therefore conceals what he has just learned. He continues to feign ignorance.

There is still another family that has responded to the appeal, so he visits them, even though it is plain to him that it no longer makes any sense. This family also realizes, as soon as they see him, that he does not belong to them. But for some reason or other, they need a male heir. So he arranges with them to pose as their son. Why? For the single reason that this would allow him to start life anew, because in this role he could again be a man without a past—only a future. Here he could be a traveler *without* luggage.

It is remarkable to see the degree to which this story agrees with the New Testament in the questions it poses, although not with its answers. It would be totally in accord with its view to say: To receive forgiveness means to obtain a new future. To receive forgiveness signifies that my baggage is taken off my back, that another has picked it up and bears it for me. For in the eyes of God I am no longer identified by my past. In simple words, this means that when God speaks of me, he does not say: "That is the person who did thus and so." He says, "That is the person for whom I plan thus and so—despite everything." The record of our debts, according to Colossians (2:14, TEV), is nailed to the cross.

Another—that is the mystery of the atonement—has assumed my burden. Now my nature is no longer determined by what is behind me, but by that which lies ahead. "The old things have disappeared . . . And now I make all things new" (Rev. 21:4,5, TEV). We are a new creation; that is the message that rings and radiates throughout the New Testament.

Naturally this liberation is totally different from that in the existentialist drama. There the past is swept away in titanic defiance. There it is renounced by brute force and deception. One acts as though it were really possible to say simply, "I am starting from scratch"—as though one could really break out of one's own identity! What will happen to that man without a memory when he launches out into the unknown in order to find a new future? The very next second he will once again be endowed with a past and be standing before the eternal eyes, laden with new baggage and new guilt. In the New Testament, on the other hand, we are told: It is the miracle of God's heart that he is not concerned with what we have been, because he has taken the burden of my life into his own heart, and because he now suffers under this burden. Golgotha is an agony in God, someone said. By that he meant that God himself bears my past, and I thus receive a new chance, a new future. That's what lies behind those old biblical words that run: "For God loved the world so much that he gave his only Son, so that everyone who believes in him may not die but have eternal life" (John 3:16, TEV).

6 *How Can Repentance Be Joyful?*

If instead of letting the yearly succession of our Christian festivals flow by heedlessly as mere routine we venture to think a little about what they mean—for example, the so-called "Day of Repentance and Prayer"*—we find ourselves feeling curiously helpless. The word "repentance" is a bad translation of the Greek idea of *metanoia*, which means something like "a change of mind." The Greek word, in turn, is a bad translation of the original Hebrew word, which means something like "turning around." We are dealing with the double breakdown of a word.

Turning to What?

Has establishing this fact helped us very much? Basically even the word "turning" doesn't contain much illuminating information about what we should do or to what we should turn. There are earnest people who cling to the prejudice that the words of an ancient tradition are both wise and useful to their lives. These earnest folks mourn the lack of substance in our culture and are therefore on the lookout for sayings that have given earlier generations power, direction, support, and comfort. They give this concept of "turning" their own meaning. They make out "turning around" to be a sort of "turning inward" to themselves. They put it this way: the hectic pace of our life-style demands a healing rest for our consciousness; it requires creative distance and composure. We are no longer in touch with ourselves; so these days I turn to myself for a change.

*The author here refers to *Buss- und Bettag* observed annually in late November by the church in Germany.

The therapeutic measures of these earnest people display an interesting and constantly recurring phenomenon: When the real purpose has been lost, that is, when the "to what" of the turning has disappeared, then we become sidetracked on the *act* of turning. People change just for the sake of changing. When people no longer know why they should believe, they become sidetracked on the act of faith and hold to "believing" as their support. When people have lost the goal, they hang on to the act of "continual striving," which is like the aimless wandering of a Faust.

We therefore—exactly like those earnest folks—misconstrue the purpose of a Day of Repentance if we understand it merely as a period of time for reflection and introspection. Actually, the point of this day is reflection *upon* something: upon the fact that our life is bogged down in details and yet only "one thing" is needed (Luke 10:42)—that we come to terms with ultimate reality. The rich farmer in Luke's Gospel (12:16ff.) had filled all his barns; he was a success, and yet by winning so much he had lost the essential ingredient in his life; he had missed obtaining peace with God. And so, the night that God demanded his life, the profit of a lifetime slipped through his fingers, and his helpless hands grasped at air. One can win the whole world and lose one's own soul. A Day of Repentance does not ask us whether we stand on our own two feet in life like a well-made, stable statue. Rather, it inquires *upon what* those feet of ours stand. It could very well be that we are standing on shaky ground. We are asked about foundations, and these foundations are offered to us.

When we overlook this question and this offer, a Day of Repentance has no meaning beyond moralism, for it is absolutely clear to us "earnest people" that we generally come up short and fail to fulfill our own goals and norms. The introspection that we do may therefore include reflection upon our shortcomings. We are quite ready to take ourselves to court. Perhaps we determine that our social structure does not remotely resemble the image of humanity which our Western tradition has held normative. Perhaps we are frightened by the degree to which we have surrendered to the fate of a mass society with its attendant breakdown of human dignity, so that an ominous tomorrow is already with us. We see the degradation of work into deadening routine; we see the dissolution of recreation into giddy amusements and distraction from the real world; we look for drugs to combat the symptoms of inadequacy and decay.

Further, it is the earnest people who seek to turn around (or turn away from) those indications of decay by a reflection on the supporting foundations of the Christian West, and particularly by a reestablishment of human dignity and its metaphysical support in the humane ideals of our tradition.

Here too, though, we ought to take seriously the objection that the so-called Christian West, together with its humane ideals, is merely a residue—I would go so far as to call it simply a "by-product"—of a proven fact: that our culture once encountered a Person who gave it its character and who provided it with a certain, even though questionable, right to call itself "Christian."

Since a Day of Repentance asks us about the proper goal of our conversion, and therefore about that Person, the decisive issue is whether we can maintain the Christian West if we lose connection with the One who supports, quickens, and fulfills it. Is it possible to hold on to certain Christian ideas of humanity, love of the neighbor, and faith, when the figure of Jesus himself has disappeared and when, instead of the original, we hold only copies of copies in our hand? Is what remains anything more than the momentum of a machine whose motor has long since been turned off and whose own stopping is just a matter of time? Are we going to be able to sustain the thesis of "the infinite value of a human soul" when the basis for that value has disappeared: namely, that the soul has been dearly bought, that the Son of God died for it, and that it therefore lives under the patronage of an eternal goodness? Will not the *value* of humanity sink to a mere *utility*? Will not human life become a means of production and a consumer product if that mainstay is removed? (We need look only to the Iron Curtain countries—though not *only* there—to see where this downhill road leads.)

Many Things Good, Yet Only One Thing Needful

At this point the theme of the Day of Repentance once again appears: that everything depends on the goal of our turnaround. If we don't want to start down that decline that has been called the road from divinity through humanity to bestiality, then it is vital for every turnaround to come to terms with that Person who sustains our life. The Day of Repentance calls us out of the moralistic details of reform measures to the "one thing" that is needful.

With splendid single-mindedness, the biblical message repeatedly concentrates the subject matter of our life on *one* point: seek first the kingdom of God, and then everything else—humanity, love of neighbor in society, a real community among peoples, the renewal of work—will be yours as well (Matt. 6:33). All these other things will *also* result as "incidentals." The opposite is true as well: if this one and only is lacking, you may build big houses, but they are built on sand; you may fill your barns, but your hands will grasp at empty air; you may stand on your own feet, but under you yawns an abyss. It would be a gain in itself if we could think of repentance relating to all the things we should achieve or do the way a mathematical sign relates to the parentheses that follow it. The significant decisions of our life are reached before we begin to remove the parentheses and total up all that our life contains.

It would, of course, be a mistake to want to take all this with deadly seriousness. Reviews—and every turnaround is certainly a review—anticipate criticism and denial. *Whether* turning around involves an act of negation depends exclusively on *where* this turning leads us. Repentance in the Christian sense is not primarily concerned with doing "better" from now on; it means returning home to him who has done all things "well." It does not mean simply to become a good person—who could seriously hope to achieve that?—but to entrust ourselves to him who is good to us. Our coming to terms with the ultimate Power that sustains our life, our making peace with it, so to speak, does not depend on our fulfilling certain conditions, on the basis of which we could become acceptable. This fulfillment of our life depends exclusively on the stand this Power takes in relation to us, and upon how it is disposed toward us.

A Guiding Ray for the Return Home

With breathtaking simplicity the Bible says that this ultimate Power is well-disposed toward us; it says that God was willing to pay a price in order to seek us out in our depths. It says that God's Son did not call to us from high overhead, but that he showed up right here where we human beings grapple with the forces of guilt, suffering, and death; and that he stood by our side, taking all that upon himself in order to be our brother.

If that is so—and in that certainty the "greats" of Christianity have always lived, in that certainty they have endured the forces of darkness, and in it they have died—then repentance is a joyous matter, because it is a return home.

> In each there lives an image
> of what we should become.
> Until we have fulfilled it
> our peace is not complete.

The return home therefore involves our destiny, what we

are supposed to be. We may enter that peace which is granted to us, when we match the pattern outlined for our lives. That, however, would spell the end to all critical negativism, that would be standing for something.

When the prodigal son we mentioned earlier decided to return home, it was not because he was weary of life in the far country; it was not because the enchantment of being in a strange land and of wallowing in his unfettered freedom gave way to satiety and a sort of hangover. Naturally ending up in a pigpen gave him an opportunity for gloomy pondering on the way his high-flying freedom had melted into nothingness, and how what he thought was "getting somewhere" now appeared as so much lost motion. The question "Where does all of this lead?" ended in a discouraging "No response." However it is not clear how this absolute bottom of his biography led to a purging, and how his dying could give rise to a rebirth. The terminal point "pigpen" is just an image for the utter nothingness to which the prodigal son saw himself abandoned; it is an endpoint in the void, an imprisonment with no way out.

The thing that raised him up was not weariness with the far country, nor was it fear of the void, nor even that he had had his fill of countless good, but fruitless, intentions. No, what gave him new initiative was recalling that his father's house was open to him, that a waiting candle burned in the window, and that he would be met by one who loved him and would recognize the failure, in all his rags, as his own flesh and blood.

Of course, it all would be a lovely fairy tale and an unreal piece of fiction if we were not permitted to know the One who gives us this story and vouches for it. Repentance is therefore not the negation of what we have behind us (or at least only in an incidental and subordinate way); rather it is the joyous breakthrough to what we have *before* us.

To receive forgiveness means that our past is crossed out and that we obtain a new future. A Day of Repentance is a festive promise that someone waits for us, and that there is always a tomorrow. The one thing that is "needful" and that therefore fills our need is this promise. Blessed are they who have a native land, for they may go home again.

7 *What Does Forgiveness Mean?*

Today there are many people who are open-minded toward religious questions even though they have no use for the church. The slogans of old-line rationalism now do their mischief principally only among the somewhat fuzzy minds of the half- (or quarter-) educated. A certain sympathy for what I might call "Christian ideals" is usually evidenced, I grant, only in regard to the fact that Christianity has social tendencies; that it includes in the widest sense, ethical standards; and that it demonstrates, through its commitment to the Absolute, a certain conservative power of inertia which is more than welcome amid the brokenness and chaos of everyday life. However, as soon as one digs deeper, the vein runs out. The figure of Jesus himself, which is the nourishing force *behind* those so-called "Christian ideals,'" appears to remain the great unknown. But then—if that is true—we must assume that the "Christian ideals" rest on a misunderstanding, that their point has been missed, and that they have been quietly transformed into the moral principles of common humanity.

Love of the Enemy

Proof that this is actually the case lies in the fact that even those groups that are well-disposed toward religion evidence no understanding of one of the central Christian ideas—love of the enemy. Isn't this demand of Jesus simply contrary to human nature? That is, doesn't it contradict the most elementary laws of nature—laws that know all about fighting and self-assertion and therefore about hostility? Doesn't

Jesus' demand arise from an infatuation with endurance, passivity, and pacifism which our healthy inner nature utterly opposes and which ultimately—if it were actually put into practice— would bring life itself to a standstill?

Now in order to understand the words correctly one must start out by realizing that this command of Jesus does not promulgate a general principle about war or about enemies of our country. Here Jesus is speaking to his disciples about those enemies who will persecute them because of their faith. He is speaking, therefore, about their personal enemies, those who do them wrong. He speaks about those enemies who later, as cruel executioners, will accompany him on his way to the cross, tormenting and mocking him, hating and attacking him.

But that does not make the problems easier by any means! How can I love anyone like that? Shall I somehow suppress and repress my natural, instinctive reactions and then, after that act of willpower, turn around and, no less powerfully, pump my system full of sympathy and feelings of love? One need only put it into words to realize that acting in such a highly unnatural way would tie a person in knots—bending over backward can be carried too far! But if loving our enemies cannot possibly be meant in that sense, how else is it to be interpreted? I would like to clarify what I mean by an example. As I recall, it was Erich Maria Remarque (author of *All Quiet on the Western Front*) who once told the following story: During the confusion of an infantry attack a soldier plunges into an out-of-the-way shell hole. There he finds a wounded enemy—either French or English. The sight of the man with his fatal wound moves him so, that he gives him a swallow from his canteen. Through this bit of human kindness a certain brotherly bond immediately springs up between them. The bond becomes deeper as they try to chat a bit. The dying man obviously wants to tell about his wife and children on whom he dwells with his last thoughts. He points to his shirt pocket. Understanding this gesture correctly, the German soldier extracts a wallet from it and then takes out a few family pictures. The gaze of the wounded man wanders over them with sadness and infinite love. The German soldier is deeply touched at that; minutes ago he would have stabbed the enemy with his bayonet; minutes ago all of his battle instincts were unleashed, as was natural in an attack. And now one of the enemy lies before him—and is no longer an enemy. No longer is he the Frenchman or the Englishman, he is simply a man, a father and a husband, one who loves and is loved, one who defended his home and who now must bid farewell to everything he holds dear. All at once the German soldier is confronted by that other man in a completely different way. It suddenly becomes clear to him that the friend/foe relationship is by no means the only one, but that behind it, or above it, there is an immediacy to the other person—who lives, as I do, in a house amid loved ones, and who, as I do, has his joys and cares.

Transformed Power

What happened in that shell hole? Did the German soldier suddenly remind himself of his duty to love his fellowman, fight back the ferocity of his battle instinct, and force himself to a gesture of human kindness? No, something quite different occurred. Instead of his having to struggle to change his own feelings, the *other* person was changed for him, and for that reason—and that reason only—he *then* changed his own way of reacting. For that reason, and that reason only, could he love the other person.

It is the same way with loving your enemy. What this act really involves can be seen best in the person of Jesus himself. How is it possible for him, the Holy One, to love the woman who was a sinner, and to pray in the presence of his executioners, "Father, forgive them, for they know not what they do" (Luke 23:34)? Could it be that his heart remained completely unperturbed by any hostile reaction to the scandal of the deceiver and adulterer, the cruelty of his tormentors, and the corruption and cowardice of Pontius Pilate? Certainly all of this must have moved him too, otherwise he would not be a human being like us. He, however, saw these hostile people not only within the coordinate system of good and evil, he saw them not only in the friend/foe relationship, but at the same time he saw them as the lost children of his Father, created for a far different fate. He sorrowed over them because they had lost their origin and their destiny. He saw in them the original divine design, to which they had been unfaithful. His all-knowing and loving eyes penetrated the outer grime and saw them as they really were.

Loving our enemies, then, does not mean that we are supposed to love the dirt in which the pearl is buried; rather it means that we love the pearl which lies in the dust. Since the people who encountered Jesus found that he uncovered this level, and they therefore did not stand before him as criminals, but as the lost and sought and mourned children of God, they were changed by those eyes. Under that gaze their original destiny revived; it was loved into being, as it were. Therefore they went away changed. God does not love us because we are by nature lovable. But we *become* lovable because he loves us.

I wanted to test out this idea, so I entrusted a strongbox to a man whose character was open to question. I thus granted him my trust although he did not in fact seem to deserve it. And the miracle happened: precisely for that reason he became trustworthy and proved himself. In forgiving and loving Jesus exercises a creative and transforming power.

That is the only way we obtain peace with God: we see that he sees something special in us. It is exactly what the father in the parable saw as his lost son returned home from the far country and approached him. He saw neither the traces of debauchery in his face nor the disreputable rags. Or better, he did indeed see all of that, but above all he saw, behind the marks of wrongdoing and under those rags, his son whom he loved.

And here is the really remarkable thing: when we realize that God looks upon us in this way, our own view of everything changes. We in turn see both neighbor and enemy in a new light. Even the boss with his temper, or the colleague who gets on our nerves with his manners, when viewed from another perspective, is entirely different from the person we see. They too are beloved and dearly bought, every one. It is amazing to discover how our relation to our surroundings changes when we take that seriously. There is a breath of something new and invigorating in our interpersonal relationships. We stand in the creative outpouring of that love with which we are loved and which then flows on from us to the other person.

At that point the self-contained world of thrust and parry, action and reaction is broken open at *one* point. A little hole has been made, so to speak, through which something completely new streams into our world. The Lord's Prayer points us to that transformed inclination when it teaches us to ask, "Forgive us our trespasses, as we forgive those who trespass against us."

8 *How Are We to Pray?*

Praying is exactly like believing: I need not be other than I am; I need only be fully who I am right now. As I am—sorrowing and needy, laughing and inclined to self-assurance—that is, in fact, the way I am to come into *God's* presence and put myself into his hands. Prayer can therefore never be conceived as a backup system for our prudence, as though *prudence* were given the task of devising tangible remedies, and *prayer* were the additional attempt to cover our flanks in the event that God might be seriously involved in it. That would be a terrible misunderstanding. To pray when in need is just the opposite of a child whistling in the dark and at the same time staring fearfully into the gloom, not knowing what menace might issue forth from it. That is not merely a psychological difference; it is bound up with the essence of prayer. To gaze into the darkness clips the wings of prayer exactly as Peter's look at the waves crippled him, even though—the parallel with prayer is exact—he wanted to hurry toward the hand of his master (Matt. 14:22–32).

The Lord's Prayer as Model for All Prayer

In this respect, the true nature of prayer—letting need be seen as need, calling hunger and fear by name, but then placing it all back in the hands of God—becomes clear in the Lord's Prayer. There, my gaze is led away from myself in a threefold manner.

First, in prayer I am not supposed to practice an art form in the sense that everything centers on my ability. For example,

I am not to "heap up empty phrases," but to "talk" as one talks with one's father. But when speaking with your father you don't look into a mirror; you direct your gaze toward *him* (Matt. 6:7).

Second, in prayer I recognize that I am not the only one in the world. I recognize that I am incorporated in the fellowship of *all* who believe and pray. That is why I say *"our* Father." This "our" indicates the twofold space in which every prayer occurs. In one sense this space—metaphorically speaking—consists of the "room" (Matt. 6:6). This metaphor hints at the *first* of the two dimensions defining my life with God.

Before God I am always, to a certain extent, "individual," and to that same extent no one can stand in my place. In the decisive matters of my life—precisely in "times of need"—I in fact stand alone. Each of us, all alone, suffers illness, has his own particular concerns, faces death, and bears his own sin. It is impossible for Adam to share his guilt with Eve, or Eve to share hers with the serpent, or for any of them simply to push it off on the others. Or rather: only One can bear all this with us and for us, and this One is not a human being as we are. Therefore this One is the only one who shares the solitude of our prayer and is with us in that "room." That is the meaning of prayer "in the name of Jesus" (John 14:13, 14; 15:16, 23, 24, 26, etc.). We could express the meaning of such prayer as follows: In that room the Word of God is with me—that judging, fatherly, self-emptying, and crucified-for-my-sake Word. I am alone with that Word. *It is the ground on which I stand and the name in which I come, when I lift my voice to pray.*

There is yet another dimension. The "room" is just a niche in the cathedral of the *whole* church, in that church which is wherever two or three are gathered "in his name," and which at the same time is the church of all believers—from the patriarchs and apostles and prophets up to the choir of those made perfect (Heb. 12:23) and to the coming kingdom beyond the boundary of our own death. What binds all these together, over and above every individual petition, is the *praise* of God. Therefore praise, strictly speaking, is *the* function of prayer, gathering the church together. In it we are one with the patriarchs, with Christians to the end of the world, and "with angels and archangels," no matter how different the content of our petitions may be. Praise bursts out of the "room"; in praise I stand in the choir of the praying church, in the choir of the holy, universal, Christian church.

That is why I begin by saying, "*our* Father." With that "our" I strike the note of praise.

Putting Ourselves into the Hands of God

Third, the above comments already hint at the last characteristic specified by the structure of the Lord's Prayer. Its petitions are set in the framework of praise. I must enter through the praise of God if I want to become a petitioner who really speaks to *God* rather than ending up somewhere else. I must praise his *name,* the coming of his *kingdom,* and the holiness of his *will* before my gaze slips back to myself and I am permitted to offer "petitions." Although those first phrases of the Lord's Prayer are called "petitions," they are really praise, since I ask God that his glory may be made known. And likewise the Lord's Prayer also ends with praise. At the conclusion my gaze wanders away from myself and turns once more to the center, so that I don't forget the giver behind the prayed for gifts, remembering that the theme of all prayer is the *hand* of God and not the *pennies* in that hand. Just as the first commandment is to shine through every individual commandment, so the individual petitions of the Lord's Prayer ought likewise to be transparent to the glory of God which is praised at the beginning and end of the prayer.

And precisely as fulfilling the individual commandments means, in essence, nothing else than "fearing and loving" God, so every individual petition of the Lord's Prayer must become a means for "praising" God. The goal of all prayer is always God himself; and if there is any standard for prayer, particularly a self-imposed standard, it should be based on this norm: *There is not only a "first commandment"; there is also a "first prayer."*

From this idea that the praise of God is the ultimate theme of all prayer, it becomes apparent that the element of *petition* in our prayers must always involve the uniting of our will with the will of God. It would be presumptuous to want to bend God's will to our own instead of uniting our will with his. That would just show that we distrusted his gracious condescension to the crib and the cross. But the Father is already constantly with us as lord and brother, with us in the depths out of which we cry. And we should unite ourselves with his will here below, where he already *is.* That is, we should trust that his will extends far above the petition and understandings of *our* will. Or better and more precisely, that it bends far down and is near us.

The petition "Thy will be done" proclaims exactly that. Granted that a limitation to our prayer, so to speak, is contained in this petition, but only in a quite specific sense. This is not an *external* limitation implying the extent to which the prayer may be fulfilled; it arises from *within,* from faith itself. Put more precisely, it means that we place our will trustfully in the hand of God and commit it to his hand, either to open up new possibilities for our praying will or to draw limits for it. The emphasis is on the "trustfully," for in that way we praise the will of God, whatever he may do with our wills. And how better could we praise him than by trusting his goodness!

After we have, as petitioners, spoken from the heart about

all that we have *on* our heart, after we have talked "as dear children with a beloved father," then we draw a heavy line, so to speak, and write beneath it, "All right, now we have said all that *we* intended. Do with it what *you* intend, for you intend good things for us and we are safe in your hands." That and nothing else is meant by "thy will be done."

9 *What Does It Mean to Take God Seriously?*

Human beings exhibit a variety of temperaments and personalities. There are thousands of gradations of faith or doubt in our encounters with God. This chapter will deal with one of these types—a widespread one—and with its representatives.

"Where Is the Proof?"

The person who asks such a question is the typical spectator who sees everything from the outside. He observes and analyzes the course of events and concludes: God is hard and unjust. He is merely the personification of fickle fate. God wants to reap where he has not sown—for example, he wants to reap *faith.* But what does he give me in order that something like faith can possibly grow in me? When I look at life that way, thinks the "spectator," it is difficult to believe that "higher thoughts" are being thought over us and that there is supposed to be a God of love. When four little children lose their mother because of a drunken driver, how can there be talk of a controlling Power? How can the note of love be sounded in even the softest tones? And how about history in the broad sense? Isn't it governed by crass interest groups or even by autonomous processes such as, say, technological development? Or the church—do its human ambiguities and its powerless pronouncements strengthen faith in any way? How can God expect to reap faith when he sows so precious little ground for it?

"Well, why take and not steal?" says the holy Johanna of the slaughterhouse in Bertolt Brecht's play. "Gentlemen," she says, "there is also a moral purchasing power. Raise the moral purchasing power and then you also have morality."

The Christian "spectator" agrees and waves resignedly: "The Lord should raise our religious purchasing power first. He should provide us with proofs of the Spirit and of his power. Then he would get all the religion he wanted, and our faith as well!"

Taking Him at His Word

One thing is sure. It is impossible to try to discover God by means of observing life, analyzing history, or the like, with the thought in mind that, should we be able to find him in that way, we would then acknowledge his existence, join his cause, and make him the norm for our life. Rather it is just the other way around: Only those who take God seriously discover him at all. There is no other way.

But how are we supposed to take God seriously if we know nothing about him? I would suggest that we deal with God exactly the way the master dealt with his servant in the parable of the talents (Luke 19:11–27). The master said to him, "I will judge you out of your own mouth." By that he means, "I encounter you and discuss with you on your own level." In exactly the same way we should say to God, "I will judge you out of your own mouth. By your own words shall you either convince me or be caught in absurdity. These words of yours tell me 'Cast all your care upon me, for I care for you' (1 Pet. 5:7). Good, I'll just do that and see if it works. I indeed have cares; I worry about tomorrow, and about next week. But for once I'm going to give up reading my daily and weekly horoscope, and instead I'll lay out these worries before you. I'm going to try you out, God. You should be worth an experiment to me. I want to see if you really get me through tomorrow and next week. I want to test out whether you really make a path for me when the way gets rough; whether you put a rod and staff in my hand when I pass through the valley of the shadow; and whether in the darkest moments, when I discern neither road nor bridges, neither shepherd nor staff, I do not lose my confidence in your guiding hand."

Taking God seriously means to take him at his word, giving him the chance to act as he has promised. When our fists are clenched or our hands hang down we can receive nothing. We must reach out our hands in request and "spread our beggar's mantle" as Luther says.

The Great Silence Broken

Maybe we need to ask, "Lord God (in case you exist), on the basis of your word (in case you said it), I ask you (in case you can hear me) to forgive my sins, be with me in my anxiety, comfort me in my loneliness, show me my neighbor, and kindle love in my heart. Let me discover that, in all good times and bad, in all the high points and frustrating times of my life, it is your hand that reaches out to me, shepherds me along, bears my burdens, strokes my brow in times of trouble, and makes death easier by cradling my head. I will get up tomorrow, making the most of my opportunities for you and serving my neighbor 'as though' you existed. Then you will break out of the great silence surrounding you and you will suddenly be with me."

That's the way it is with God. When we listen, God speaks; when we obey, God acts. "He who comes to me I will not cast out," says Jesus Christ (John 6:37). He died for those words. He took us that seriously. He deserves our giving him a chance.

10 *What Is Trust?*

I would like to quote some sections from a letter which I wrote to a young soldier during World War II. He had gone through many terrible experiences, and a grisly mask was slowly but surely interposing itself before the face of the Father in whom he had previously believed. He was obsessed with the question, "How can God let that happen?" That was the theme of our correspondence with one another. A section of one of my letters goes as follows:

Are you acquainted with Faust's experience on Easter eve, when he had put the cup of poison to his lips, frightened to death of the doubt and desperation that welled up in his heart? Then he heard the sound of the Easter bells, and that sound came to him like a liberating message, like the word of one who puts a hand on his shoulder and tells him, "You are not supposed to die; God has thrown open heaven."

What Faust experienced figuratively and distantly has come near to the Christian as the loving voice of God. Of course, that voice does not descend miraculously out of the clouds but is embedded in the word of a fellow human who is empowered to tell me in God's stead, "I have called you by name, you are mine" (Isa. 43:1), thereby coming to meet me and placing my hand into the hand of God. At such times it is more apparent than usual that God's voice does not originate in the distant past. It is not some pious tradition reeking of age. It is spoken *now* and my fellow human being has *just* brought it from heaven; it still rings with the sound of God's voice.

Perhaps we can only grasp this word spoken *now* and to *us* when we ponder the miracle of Christmas. As God became human in the mystery of that holy night, so he sends down his word ever anew, becoming a human word. The "brother or sister in Christ" bears this word in hand and mouth and now I apply it to myself and let it be said to me, exactly as Simeon took the child Jesus in his arms, holding the heavenly blessing lovingly in his hands.

"In death, in the abyss, and in doubt we should remind ourselves," said Luther, "I have the word that I *shall* live no matter how hard death may press me." Grasp that, dear friend, "I *have* the word." I hold it in my hands; it is spoken to me now! So I don't need to say anymore, "Somewhere I once heard a word. It seems to me that something like that existed." No, I *have* the word. It strikes my ears now.

It strikes me so personally that it uses no formal type of address, nor does it talk in generalities about the destiny of mankind as philosophical systems do. No, this word says to me: You shall live—you, specifically. But even *that* is probably put too inadequately and weakly. I am not addressed by an "it." A brother or sister, and through that person God himself, speaks to me. I can now say with Luther, "Death doesn't matter. The Lord has promised me that I *shall* live. That I believe."

When I read those words of Luther, closing with that defiant "That I believe" like the period at the end of a sentence, it sounds to me almost like a resolution. "That's that. Now God has the responsibility for what he has said—and for my faith, too. Everything becomes one big blur to me—especially my pious intentions. The only point of reference is that word 'You shall live.' I stake everything on that one card. God asserts that he has you in his hand. Therefore, he is the one who is responsible. In his name I throw myself into the night, hoping that I fall into the hands of God."

That is what the concluding phrase "That I believe" sounds like. I could even say that it appears to be a signature written with such a defiant flourish that the ink spills. However, if we call it a signature, it is really only a *countersignature,* a countersignature, executed blindfolded and with immense scrawls, to the promise that God signed and sealed with blood—the promise that I shall live.

Dear friend, do you still remember what you wrote in your first letter about sometimes closing your eyes and playing dead the way an animal does? That was in connection with the shelling and the moments of greatest danger. You said that such actions were neither cowardly nor just hiding your head in the sand. Notice that *faith* too has such moments when it closes its eyes and lets itself fall, knowing that it will end up either in the abyss or in the hands of God. It dares to leap on account of the simple words "My hand, my hand," knowing in spite of everything that the journey cannot end in the abyss, but only in those hands.

Don't get me wrong, K____! In no case is it correct to say that we must become blind in order to believe. We must conclude precisely the opposite—that faith is coupled with the clearest perception available to us human beings—the clear perception and realism of people in the Bible. The fact is that faith *equips* our eyes and teaches them to recognize things about us, and around us, and above us that are concealed from their natural powers. We need to remind ourselves, however, that the eyes do not see by their own light, but that the light is borrowed, a gleam illuminated by the thoughts of God himself (Ps. 36:9). To keep us mindful of this fact, I believe, our eyes must always become darkened and die, experiencing the death and change known to every Christian. We have the promise that, as Christians, we shall become the most clear-sighted of humankind, permitted to know the mysteries of God. But this clear-sightedness comes into being only from those eyes that renounce every claim. It arises among those who dare to become blind because they know that eyes are watching over them that take no pleasure in that arrogant look of humankind as it loses God's worldwide strategy among parochial perspectives and usurps the honor of being a part of his government.

You see, dear friend, since all that is true, and since our eyes are basically domineering and anti-godly, then their light must die out if they want to see the light of God. Therefore, they must enter through "blind" faith. It appears to me that blind people who received their sight from Jesus saw *more* of his glory than did the hawk-like eyes of all the kind and the critical spectators put together. Granted, even those blind eyes that God illuminated could not know all the secrets of Christ. Perhaps they were opened wide a short time later, startled as they watched the events on Golgotha. Perhaps just behind them the brain was asking in dark despair, "How can God let this happen?" Perhaps, perhaps. For even the eyes that have become clear and capable of sight are not yet "seeing" eyes on that account; they belong to those who walk by faith and not by sight. They belong to those who each day graft afresh their petitions and understanding into the will of God, even if soul and mind and intellect might protest. That alone is called trust; that's what faith means.

Now it has become late, dear friend, and I am walking on the veranda to get a little air. The lightless, blacked out plain along the Rhine lies at my feet. Many soldiers have made agreements with those they left at home to look up at the stars at night so that their gazes can meet at some distant point. Perhaps you are also looking upward at this same moment.

But I see nothing as yet. The sky is black and dark, although I know that it is cloudless. The glow of my desk lamp is still affecting my eyes. We don't see the sky as long as human lights dominate our vision. In a moment or two these lights will die away. Then the stars will become visible; first the bright ones, and afterward the more distant ones, across space that my mind cannot measure. Finally, the wonder of the heavens will be spread out above me, and I dimly realize that there are still many stars and distances up there that I cannot see. But they exist under the same heaven, and there are eyes that have counted them and that know all about them.

11 *Who Is My Neighbor?*

How could people give pastoral care to Nazi war criminals after World War II, and how can people visit terrorists and murderers in their cells today?

Pastoral care obviously has something to do with *love.* It seeks the strayed, the trapped, and the guilty because the "well have no need of a physician" (Matt. 9:12).

If you do not understand the essence of the love that Jesus preached and praised you can't explain to yourself why anyone would visit a war criminal or a terrorist. You would either consider the visitor a sympathizer with the prisoner or, even worse, an emasculated, indifferent being for whom all alternatives are reduced to a mishmash and all contrasts are blurred.

So the decisive question is: How do I understand that love which seeks the lost, the strayed, and the trapped? Here are just two of its characteristics.

First. In general we human beings live according to the law of the echo principle—what you do to me, I do to you. Whoever serves our interests is our friend; whoever is against them counts as enemy or at least as opponent. We behave "reactively." Thus there follows a tendency toward heightening the differences. We are caught in this vicious circle. It is operative in a quarrel over a lease, and in tensions between ideologies and entire nations. It seems to belong to the nature of our world.

Jesus, however, exists literally "outside the framework" of the world, because he broke through this vicious circle. He is the liberator, because he freed himself and those who belong to him from this curse. He teaches us that loving only those who love us is not enough because then we are still merely on the "reactive" level and have not gotten off the merry-go-round. Instead he takes the *initiative* and makes a new beginning. The other person must not first *be* lovable in order to share in Jesus' love. This love of his is "prevenient," it is prior to the other's. But precisely for that reason it releases the other's love and opens it up. It could be that it thus *makes* the other lovable. Therefore his love is not reactive, but creative. It gives a fresh start. It breaks the curse caused by conflicts of interest and aggression.

We can observe the same process occurring when it comes to *trust.* A group of my students are concerned about released prisoners. Society usually receives parolees with mistrust, tries to keep them at arm's length and thus consigns them again to a life of crime. According to the reaction principle that is quite natural: our trust is usually the response to *trustworthiness* that is already present, and trustworthiness is precisely what the parolees can *not* offer.

Trust has a different aspect when it is seen as a part of the love taught by Jesus. It is a trust that takes the initiative. It is risked and applied to someone who doesn't yet seem to be trustworthy at all. But now that person can become so, because the joy of receiving trust reopens the clogged springs of humanity. Here again a vicious circle is broken. Here again a creative newness is at work in the world. God certainly "first" loved us (1 John 4:19) before we were worthy of that love—or ever are. As at a candle-lighting service, age after age has kindled something new by touching the candle of that first Christmas.

Second. As a rule we human beings tend to identify our opponent with an opposition group. He or she belongs to the "other" party, or is my opposite number in wage negotiations; he or she is "the" Arab, "the" Israeli, "the" Communist, "the" capitalist. Here, in the bud, is the same tendency that political fanatics take to the extreme: only the people of my point of view are "human," the others are "pigs" or "Reds." When we hear it like that, it sounds like gutter language, barbaric and coarse, but it is just the final stages of a process that begins when we look upon living persons as simply bearers of some banner, or as representatives of some movement. When we do that we demote them to the rank of mere tools.

Of course, when it came to evil Jesus called a spade a spade. (He was, in fact, recklessly blunt about it.) But he grieved over those upon whom evil lay like a curse, and he broke their fetters. Even while he hung on the cross, he still prayed for the executioners and the blasphemous slanderers who stood there watching the execution. He saw even the rough dice-throwing soldiers as more than mere representatives of a "counter-ideology" of which he himself was a victim. Instead, he was troubled about their lost souls, about their blindness, and about their being untrue to their *proper* destiny. He still saw them as children of his Father in heaven who wandered unaware in an alien land and thereby fell prey to self-alienation at the same time. Therefore even in dying he managed to utter a last plea for his persecutors.

The love that Jesus taught and lived lifts us to a new dimension. It lets us see our fellow human beings as more than tools in the service of interests that either work *for* us or are directed *against* us. We can see them as children of our Father in heaven, of value to him and also of concern to us.

That is the new note that is sounded for the first time in the gospel. That is the light that shone in the darkness (John 1:5). From this point on there is no human being who is not called by name—by *name* and not by the cause or the movement which that person represents. We are now related to God "directly." That constitutes our worth. God does not love us because we are so worthy, but we are worthy because God loves us.

The implications of this relationship are tremendous. But how few people understand the presupposition on which they are based!

12 *What Is Our Relationship with the Animal World?*

An Unwritten Chapter of the Doctrine of Creation

When I heard that there was a dog in Sputnik II, I held a silent conversation with my dachshund. At first I addressed him as the individual dog named "Axel" with whom my children play and from whom, after every trip, I get an overwhelming reception of unrestrained joy—a joy that is a bit reminiscent of Eden. In that frame of mind I thought, "How lucky that they didn't launch you up there, and that you are still here with us."

But then, beneath my hand, he became a representative of his entire species. He belongs to that class of beings who have established a bond with humanity and have become our friends. Sometimes I am troubled by the fact that we Christians speak so little about faithfulness to the creation upon which God lets his sun shine and his rain fall. He is not only Lord of the good and evil, but also Lord of that which lies beyond good and evil. And if love is something that gives itself and pities the weak, then certainly it also includes love for a helpless creation.

For the greatness of humanity, to which we are called and which gives us dominion over the earth, is not to manifest itself in brutal *exploitation* of the creation (one need think only of egg-laying factories) but in a *consideration* for it (Gen. 1:27–28; 2:19). This consideration consists in humanity's self-knowledge—that we can attain our destiny or that we can lose it, and that we may relate to him who gives life (Gen.

2:16). That is just what the rest of creation neither knows nor can do. Because human beings, however, do know and have the ability, because we may look up to our creator, the rest of creation becomes like a talent entrusted to us.

"The man gave names to all cattle, and to the fowl of the air, and to every beast of the field" (Gen. 2:20), says the creation account. Its intention is clearly to say that the man also *called* the animals by these names. There was a sort of community with them. In a healthy world, all created beings are together under God. Humanity stands under God consciously; the animals unconsciously. This talent of consideration, given and entrusted to humanity, cannot be turned *against* those who are subordinated and subjected to us. For if we exercise our dominion in the name of God, we can only exercise it in the name of that love which drives us beyond ourselves, and in the name of that fostering care which God devotes to *all* his creation.

But *is* the world still healthy? And if it is not—if the world of humanity lies in twilight, if the grasp for the forbidden fruit, if Cain's murder of his brother, and the building of the tower of Babel have cast a pall over the dawn of creation—how does that affect the creatures who yet stand on the other side of good and evil? Are not the animals drawn into this?

Paul once used the enigmatic phrase "groaning of the creation" (Rom. 8:22) and indicated that it too cried out for redemption. This is not the place to go into what is meant by that phrase. It involves the ultimate mysteries. I will only describe how the phrase took on meaning for me personally.

Once when I was a young man—before I concerned myself with the theological dimensions of that obscure phrase—I asked an elderly servant of God how he made sense out of it. He simply said, "Look a dog in the eye, then you will know."

Now, I don't believe for a minute that he gave me an adequate explanation of that phrase, but since that time I have never ceased to ponder what he said. When I look at a dog, and he looks at me, those words come back again and again. And although one must guard against sentimentality and reading too much into the situation, I nevertheless cannot shake the feeling that a real dialogue with the creation takes place. And this is the way it sounds:

"My little canine friend, you are just one particular part of creation. The two of us—in contrast to innumerable fellow creatures of yours—have been brought together in a remarkable way and live with one another. If something bad would happen to you, I would be very upset. And I know that if something would happen to me, that your canine heart would be affected. You notice at once if something is bothering me. And if I am happy, then you make the most droll attempts to show me that you rejoice with me. Sometimes the riddle of creation gazes at me from your eyes so powerfully, so terribly, that it penetrates me through and through. I imagine that you suffer under the burden of not being able to express yourself and to tell me what you know. Of course you can be very expressive with your many bodily motions, with your tail wagging and even with your little paws. But speaking is just out of the question. Sometimes you let me know that I don't understand you. There is a very deep gulf between us that neither of us can cross. And precisely because you are such a unique part of creation, because you have bound your canine destiny to me, a human being, this limitation becomes particularly painful. Our lives are more fully linked than I can say or you can bark. You are a dumb creature, and maybe you are thinking, 'My master is a noseless creature.'"

Sometimes a dog can even preach you a sermon. And it is not far behind the sermon which, according to Jesus, even little children can preach. I experienced that on a ship while I was enroute to the United States.

On the way over there was a large German shepherd on

board whose master had placed him in the care of the crew, because he himself wanted to go by air. That was a very miserable dog. He lived in an unfamiliar world with strange scents and strange people that were totally foreign to him. The floor rocked, there were no trees, and at the railing the world came to an end. That was truly, as the existentialists would say, "being thrown into nothingness"; his entire canine world view collapsed, and he plunged into emptiness and the void. The groaning of the creation was no longer a figure of speech when one looked at that dog.

On the return trip we also had a dog along. He was a lap-dog, a mere "half-pint." Even though the external circumstances were exactly the same for him as for the other dog, there were *no* waves of sadness emanating from him. His master was beside him. The little creature often gazed up at him as if to say, "This is a crazy world; I have stopped trying to figure it out, but if you are along things can't really be that bad. Sooner or later all this nonsense will stop and then I will once more sniff halfway normal smells and find trees that I can enjoy." Precisely because a sort of friendship exists between man and beast, that little animal could preach an impressive sermon on trust.

Suffering and Death for Human Beings

Another consequence of this superiority of human beings is that we are embarrassed when animals must suffer for us—no matter whether it is an old cart horse, a watchdog, or a small animal used in space research. I'm not talking about the painful struggle and the fear in nature itself. That deserves a chapter of its own. I am talking only about the pain that human beings inflict on their animals.

Why are we ashamed of ourselves when we kill animals, perform experiments on them, and cause them to suffer for us? Obviously because an animal cannot suffer "ethically." We humans can give some meaning to our suffering. And even when we can't understand it—in contrast to a martyr, for example, who is privileged to understand why he or she is suffering—the pain nevertheless becomes a school for us, in which we learn to rely upon the "higher thoughts" of God. An animal, however, suffers without the consolation of either understanding or trust.

Of course, we must not become sentimental. An animal's pain is certainly far different from ours. Precisely because the creature does not understand, it knows nothing of the future, but lives in the present moment. Therefore it is spared the complete fullness of pain that we humans suffer as we await future agonies, tormented by our finitude. And yet, even if the pain of animals is concentrated only in the immediate and clear-cut moment (a cow goes on eating after being momentarily frightened by a thunderclap), this moment is nevertheless filled with the whole burden of meaningless pain and puts an end to creaturely comfort. And we humans have done that to them.

Perhaps the feeling of shame that comes over us in such cases is the last remnant of a pious modesty that shrank from doing anything that would injure the creation. It is also the last symptom of a consciousness that the world is no longer intact and that a great fissure runs not only through the human world, with its distress, hostility, exploitation, and uneasiness, but that this fissure dominates the rest of creation as well.

Only a person who knows something about the fall of humanity and its continuing effects can rightly comprehend why things are like this. Such a person also knows why it is that, in this world edging toward chaos, we cannot renounce the use of force, punishment, confinement, and the inflicting of pain. The very existence of the state with its compulsory structuring of self-assertion is an example of this sort of emergency measure in the fallen world. In this questionable world the good will survive only if it wears armor. If one removed its powers of vengeance, the legions of evil would raise their impudent heads and chaos would close in on us.

This is how we survive in a world of conflicts. Only a dreamer can fail to see that. And it is a sign of God's grace that he has espoused these emergency measures and has stretched the rainbow of his promise over the world, questionable though it has become; further, he lets it all continue until it will reach the "last day."

It would therefore be a mistake to use Albert Schweitzer's beautiful phrase about "reverence for life" in a sentimental and unrealistic way. Exactly as it is impossible for us humans to live together in society without making sacrifice, it is also impossible to live with the rest of creation without sacrifice. There is no way around the fact that animals must die in order to maintain human life. Having admitted that, however, we should never fail to tremble at the brokenness of creation, where one must suffer if another wishes to get ahead.

The bodies of horses strewn over the battlefields of mankind constitute an indictment that innocent creatures have been dragged into human strife. And it is significant that the shame and sorrow it arouses is not totally stifled, even when there is no way to spare the creation its misery between the fall and the last judgment. It means that at least somewhere within us a spark remains of the knowledge that humanity, although ruler of the world, does not have the *right* to treat the creation so, but that treatment of that sort is our *basic fault*, and that it is the source of the disorder which threatens the whole universe.

A Tainted Love for Animals

There is also a perverse love of animals by which we dishonor them. One's love of animals can be "sectarian," so to speak—a pseudo-religion. That is invariably the case when we misuse animals to hoodwink ourselves and others for example, by cultivating an indulgent love of animals and on that account letting our fellow humans starve. We thus substitute cheap emotionalism for a sacrificial attitude.

There is a love of animals that is the sign of an extreme degeneracy. This degeneracy consists in our no longer being capable of real love; perhaps we even despise human beings and consequently idolize animals. When I see or read about someone who serves a lapdog choice steaks and other human food on a silver tray or—as sometimes in the United States—puts up an elegant tombstone in a pet cemetery, I am inclined to diagnose it as a symptom that the person lacks communication with others and has lost touch with fellow humans. Usually, when I have pursued the matter, I have found that to be the case.

Animals remind us of an unfallen world where Adam gave names to his brothers and sisters in creation, and conversed with them. They remind us of a world once again called into being when Francis of Assisi preached to the birds as his beloved fellow creatures.

13 *How Do We Get Rid of Our Rabbits' Feet?*

A few years ago, after lecturing on some religious subject, I was to be taken back home by car. The driver of the automobile knew that I had given that lecture, and before we had traveled a mile he felt obligated to say, "Doctor, you're a theologian, aren't you? I'm sorry to say that I myself don't believe in anything."

I responded, "You didn't even have to tell me that. I noticed it as soon as I got in your car." The honest driver was obviously so floored by this answer that I momentarily feared for his steering; he turned toward me abruptly and asked, slightly disconcerted, "How did you figure that out?"

"Well," I replied, "when I saw your various good luck charms and talismans dangling there, I knew that you didn't believe in God and therefore were dragging yourself around with a corresponding amount of anxiety."

"To be frank with you," he stated, "I don't quite get the connection." Yet the whole matter seemed to be rather intriguing to him.

A System of Superstitious Protection

"I'll be glad to tell you my idea about the connection," I answered. "If you don't believe in God, you no longer know about the fatherly backdrop for the world. Everything—your personal life as well as all of world history—dissolves into the workings of blind forces and meaningless accidents. And so the world itself becomes sinister to you. It becomes downright hostile. Every tree along this boulevard is your secret enemy, because it could dent your radiator. And every truck is an evil and incalculable monster that could come too close to your scalp. So you see, you need to protect yourself against this sinister world that you mistrust. Therefore the good luck charms."

My driver was a serious and reflective man. It especially impressed me that, at first, he said nothing. Clearly, conflicting thoughts were battling within him. He then disclosed to me that he had, in fact, worked out an entire protective system of supersitition and had built it up around his life like a strategic belt of fortifications. He confessed with comforting openness that it all really expressed a sort of defensive posture against the uncertainties and hard knocks of life. "There is the competitive crunch," he said, "and the uncontrollable influences on my growing children. There are threats to health, and the many other things that make a person uneasy."

Dark Powers in the Background

All of that, however, did not come out at once; it came gradually and bit by bit over the course of a whole hour. As he thus spoke on, he seemed to me to be representative of all humanity, just as it comes to expression in the classic statue of Laocoon—a man trying to defend himself from the coils of serpents—or in the Germanic myth of the Midgard saga, where the world is seen as encircled by a snake. (We have discussed that above.)

It is the world in which spring and winter occur, in which festivals are celebrated and pain endured, the scene of birth and death. But on the horizon is the power of the sinister; in the farthest background lurk the dark, destructive forces. "Snatch the light from the jaws of the serpent," said the German poet-physician, Hans Carossa, as he commends life and life-affirmation to us. Let the little lamps shine before the darkness from the edge of the world creeps in upon us!

Then Are Christians Free from Worry?

"Do you really think, then," asked the man after a period of silence, "that the Christian experiences the world differently? Is the Christian free from worry? How about you, for example, don't you worry?"

That was really a question of conscience, and I dared not present myself as better than I was.

"Of course, I know worry as well as you do."

"Well," he observed, "it is comforting, frankly, that you aren't any better off." He ceremoniously took a deep breath. "But in general," he continued, "Christians always act as though they were slightly special. Such hypocrisy was always irritating to me." That started him talking for quite a while. He bubbled over with graphic and unpleasant instances which he had experienced.

"Wait a minute," I interjected at that point, "I believe you have missed my point. We Christians are indeed a little different—or supposed to be, at any rate."

"Aha, I thought so!" he crowed, but immediately tried to pull back tactfully: "Well, of course, otherwise there wouldn't be any point to all that nonsense if something better didn't come out of it."

I didn't dare let him win so cheap a victory. "Look," I said, "earlier in your life you surely learned Jesus' statement, 'In the world you have tribulations, but be of good cheer, I have overcome the world'" (John 16:33, RSV).

"I did learn it, but frankly, I never understood it."

I then gave my driver a little exposition of those words. It took many miles and a lot of conversation, which I will summarize here in a few sentences.

Of course, if you are a Christian, you have problems in this world, exactly as other folks do. However, you deal with these worries differently. You need not repress them nor superstitiously exorcise them. You have with you him who has overcome this worrisome world with the serpent on its horizon.

Then what is the significance of having overcome the world through this One? It means, first, that he is with us. I know no better summary of the gospel than the fact that he is *with* us: throughout his whole life he was to be found with the sick, the lonely, and the guilty. And finally he even met his end in our human death—not triumphantly, by the way, as though it didn't matter to him, but so totally that he called out in despair to his Father because he no longer could see his face.

With Us, Besieged by Death

When we Christians say that this One has overcome guilt and death, we often make that confession far too lightly. Frequently we say (and think), "After all, he was almighty. He simply called off the angel of death; he didn't let him 'get to him.'"

On the contrary, Jesus felt the pain of a refugee's life, of loneliness, and of death, and he lay in exactly the same grave in which we all shall one day lie. He has also been imprisoned; he too has fallen into the hands of men. He too has been treated meanly. He has indeed let all that "get to him." Otherwise he would never be our companion and our brother.

I want to put that in an image. We are encircled by enemy powers. We are somewhat like soldiers in wartime who are surrounded. He does not call off those besieging powers by virtue of some sort of omnipotence; he lands in the middle with us. He takes the worry and the privation of the besieged upon himself, and breaks the blockade from within. Note that—from within. In temptation he faced sin exactly as we do; the devil tried to hoodwink and hypnotize him too. But he took care of that. He walked down the dark passage of death, but he crashed through the final wall; he blew away the stone which covered his grave. Thus he takes with him those who walk at his side and leads them through the loneliness of their last hour. He does not spare us from death. But he goes along. He doesn't spare us from the world and its sinister ends either. But he is with us during the siege.

We wander through this remarkable and incalculable life as though it were a valley of shadows. We have no promise that we will be led around it, but we have someone beside us. We are not left alone.

We are like children in a darkening forest. The moonlight creates bizarre shadows. Sinister noises reach our ears. But we are protected by a hand which has drawn an invisible circle around us, and the sinister forces can no longer clutch at us. Even the thought that we are not worthy of this Lord can no longer distress us.

14 *Is History the Final Judgment?*

The Absurd in History

How often we are plagued by the thought that history doesn't turn out properly. It is the heavier firepower that wins—not the right! How can we explain the way ideological tyranny openly survives without any likelihood of being cast into the abyss by a hand from on high? How can God let that happen? This agonizing question comes up constantly. Is world history *(Weltgeschichte)* really, as Schiller said, the final judgment *(Weltgericht)* ? Or is our recording of history nothing more than "giving meaning to the meaningless," as Theodor Lessing once put it? If, however, there is no divine judgment and no meaningful direction to history, can there then be a *God*?

Now it's true—and the experience of people in biblical times confirms it—that there is no easy way to establish objectively what the judgment of God really is. We can clarify that by an example:

There is a song about the destruction of Napoleon's army in Russia:

> The Lord has smitten them indeed
> By striking man and cart and steed.

Does this actually involve an unambiguous judgment of God against Napoleon? Couldn't a Frenchman object, and with justification, that the exact opposite is true—that it was Europe and not Napoleon which was smitten by God, since that defeat deprived Europe of Napoleon's organizing genius and its benefits? And doesn't that judgment make Napoleon merely an executioner? The character of great figures is not the only image that wavers in history; the role assigned to them by divine governance of the world is obviously ambiguous as well.

In our personal lives, too, the diagnosis that certain events, troubles, and catastrophes are the "judgment of God" always comes up against a final limit which calls it into question: Must I interpret the suffering which I undergo from inoperable cancer, for instance, as directly traceable to previous guilt and therefore as the judgment of God? Isn't it also possible to explain it in terms of its goal, namely, God's *instructing* purpose, and wouldn't these two opposite interpretations of suffering cancel out each other? In the account of the man born blind (John 9, especially vv. 1–3) these two interpretations of suffering dramatically collide in the conversation of Jesus with the disciples. The disciples make, for them, the obvious assumption that a sin must be the root cause for this penalty of congenital blindness; that either the afflicted man or his parents must have sinned. To the contrary, Jesus rejects this explanation of the disciples, and apparently turns it completely around. He says that the blindness of this poor man makes sense because God's power will be seen at work in him. Thus, in the same way, when cares and catastrophes strike our lives it is not enough to ask *why* did this happen to me, but also *for what purpose* do I suffer this hard fate?

The Silent Judgment

In any event, it is not easy to establish a clear connection between suffering and sin. Because it is so difficult for us to establish the relationship between guilt and punishment, at least in many cases, we are continually forced to the question, why is God silent? Why does he remain passive when, according to our expectation, he should come down in a storm of judgment and set things straight? This sort of question tends to be especially vexing for pious folk.

It is by no means true, however, that *nothing* at all happens when God seems to be silent and inactive. It is precisely in his silence and inactivity that the judgment can be carried out—in fact it can even *be* the judgment. In the language of faith this means that God withdraws his hand and leaves humanity to its own devices, that he gives them over to the consequences of their deeds and thereby delivers them to self-judgment. Precisely in the moment when, since God is silent, the godless feel secure and deride the divine judgment because they confuse the apparent act of divine permissiveness with the non-existence of God, precisely in that moment the believer can see the judgment of God looming over the world like a gripping nightmare. This feeling can master him so strongly that he can welcome the storm of wrath when it breaks loose as a liberation from the ghastliness of the silent judgment. *Dieu se retire*—God withdraws (compare Hos. 5:15 to 6:3).

Thus we see that the apparent silence of God toward the world, the apparent non-fulfillment of judgment, should not be attributed to a mere lack of antennae on humanity's part for the inner connection, as though the silence of God were only an acoustical problem, not audible to our deaf ears and hardened hearts. In other words, the judge's silence is not merely related to the insensitivity of our hearts.

No, the judge's silence is an objective fact. It belongs to the authentic "style" of divine judgment. Even the angels who stand about God's throne can testify to the reality of God's silence. It does not stem from the insensitivity of human beings at all. God can actually be silent. He judges not only—or rather, he hardly ever judges—by striking the offenders with his lightning bolt or some other catastrophe. He judges by silently "letting be." That is the way he let the people who built the tower of Babel fail through their own godlessness. By doing nothing, so to speak, he let them in their godlessness end up being scattered. Thus his silence was supreme action. What he let happen there amounted to a coming down and confusing of things. God was active in their self-confusion—by "looking on." In the same way he has "given up" the unbelievers, the escapists, to their own wretchedness (Rom. 1:18ff.).

This giving up and turning over (the Greek is *paradidōmi)* is the method of the silent judgment, even though one could momentarily suppose that this was merely the general law of guilt-atonement coming to light.

Thus we begin to understand why it is always so difficult to establish a connection between guilt and punishment in history. It is necessary to know the *judge* in order to understand his verdicts. As long as we do not relate to the personal "you" of this judge who appears in Jesus as our Father, we are thrown hopelessly up against the question of how order is maintained in the world. This quandary is actually "hopeless" in the strict sense of the word; not only because the agonizing question of "why" cannot be laid to rest, but also because this "why" question cannot be resolved, for it remains "unredeemed."

This lack of redemption expresses itself basically in two directions. In one form the "why" question ends in a blind alley, in the cold comfort of declaring it to be unfathomable. The next step beyond this assertion of unfathomability leads to the nihilistic view that the apparently unfathomable has, in fact, no bottom; that the world is therefore without governance, that it is without a Father. The second form of the "why" question ends in the statistical perspective of "the greatest good for the greatest number"—the assertion of an icy legalism and the impersonal silence of nature. A combination of the first and second answers occurs in the attempt to understand the finite world as "tragic." That means to assert that there is an order, a destiny, which cannot be questioned by gods or by men. One does not know by *whom* this destiny is controlled, nor to *what end. This situation, in which the judgment is no longer understood, because the judge is no longer known, is itself judgment.*

Redemption from the "Why" Question

The biblical message proclaims redemption from the blind alley of this problem of meaning, this painful puzzle of history with its hidden judgments. That redemption consists, not in a solution to the "why" question, but in turning it into the "for what" question.

Once again I recall the account of the man born blind. The disciples ask, "Why was this man born blind? Who has sinned?" Jesus, on the other hand, asks "For what has this suffering been imposed?" in order to answer, "So that God's power might be seen at work in him" (John 9:3). The "why" question is directed backwards toward the past seeking to fathom the cause. It wants to reach the answer: "Therefore, since thus-and-so, God did this and that." But this answer is not forthcoming. It is concealed in a higher counsel. The "for what" question, on the other hand, rejects that answer; it is secure in the certainty that we can let ourselves be surprised, because we are protected. Neither the satanic nor the senseless looms on the horizon; a fatherly basis undergirds the world. Thus, faced with the riddle of history, the Christian does not say, "Therefore, since. . . "; but rather, "*Nevertheless* I am continually with thee" (Ps. 73:23). That is because the Christian sees judgment from the judge's point of view. The judge, however, is none other than the Father upon whom we may call and whose children Jesus Christ has made certain we are.

The face of this judge will appear at the Last Judgment. Joseph Wittig once said that a biography ought really to begin with death rather than birth; it can be written only from the end back towards the beginning, because only at the end can the totality of a life become visible in its fulfillment. The same is true for history.

Only when the final hour of the world has struck, that hour of the second Advent, when faith may see what it has believed and when unbelief *must* face what it has *not* believed—only this final hour will disclose the secret meaning of history, the true biography of the world.

15 *Death and Life*

On one of the first pages of the Högfeld Book, a book published in 1938 by Hogfeld, a Swedish painter who was particularly known for his humorous pictures, there is a striking illustration. Amid mandolins and Chinese lanterns, a jolly group floats along on their boat. As they glide on the river, beasts of prey with burning eyes slink through the night on both banks, waiting for the group to step ashore. No matter how ravenously those eyes shine through the darkness, the joyful singers and tipplers, surrounded by lanterns and mandolins, pay no attention to the threatening danger. When it comes right down to it, almost all of us travel that way, enjoying life "as long as the lanterns glow."

Death Displaced

Ought I begin by pointing out *why* we hear and see nothing? We all are familiar with that lulling mandolin music, that siren song of a false conquest of death that does nothing but "triumphantly" dismiss this "last enemy." It says that there is only the natural cycle of spring, summer, autumn, and winter, the rhythm of eternal coming and going. Death, it says, is nothing but the downbeat in this rhythm of life. It is all so natural that there is no need to fret about it.

New Year's Eve customs are also revealing in this connection. Why is it that people have to drink, shoot, shout, and sing? Perhaps they have to *over*-sing, *over*-shout, and become *over*-loud because in this last night of the year they hear Father Time sharpening his scythe, and they want to drown out that sound because they cannot bear it. Is it really just the natural rhythm of time, continually reminding us of the end, death, and passing of all things human? It is, however, remarkable to observe how few physicians there are who would dare to tell a dying person how completely "natural" a process lay immediately before him. What keeps us from speaking about these "natural" things? Why must we lie and cover up *if* they are really so natural? Or is it possible that something quite different from what we think becomes visible beyond death?

Recently I read the following account in the diary of a young flyer who had been killed. He wanted to pick a bouquet of lilacs, and as he bent away the branches he found the half-decayed body of a soldier under the blooming bush. He jumped back—not because he had never seen a dead man before—he jumped back because the contrast between the dead man and the flowering bush cried out at him. Had he come upon a withered lilac bush, he would not have been so shocked. A blooming lilac would also one day become wilted—that is really just an expression of the rhythm of life. But that a human in that decayed state should be lying under a bush in full flower just wouldn't fit. *That* was the reason he drew back. He had sensed that this dead comrade somehow was in contradiction to the creator's plan for life. He had sensed that the dead man lay as a foreign object in the blooming realm of creation. It had given him an intimation that death is something un-natural to humanity. All things considered, this young airman was already closer to the world of the New Testament and its message about death than are the people who constantly prattle about the "naturalness" of human death.

Before us rises the image of the Lord, as he goes through the countryside, healing the sick, laying his reassuring hand on the afflicted and the heavyhearted, forgiving sins, and raising the dead. If we take a closer look at this picture of the healing and forgiving Son of God, we discover that the New Testament figuratively sees this whole world with its disorder, guilt and death, and its suffering and tears as one totality. Here sins, guilt, suffering, sickness, and death all belong together. They are different aspects of a world off the track, a world out of joint.

Death as Unnatural

Thus for Jesus, too, death is not just a natural conclusion to life. It is *not* natural and in order. It is not willed by God, when this grim reaper comes and simply breaks the bonds of friendship, marriage, and love. This grim reaper may not simply come and break into God's created world. It was this incarnate monstrosity, this "disorder," that the young flyer's boyish instinct had detected.

The Bible makes this crystal clear. The death of human beings points to an ultimate disorder. It should *not* be, the grim boundary markers should *not* stand between us and the eternal life of God. And precisely for that reason this whole unnatural state, the disorder, this "brokenness" of the world give way when Jesus Christ comes and lays his ordering and healing hand on his fellow humans.

Yet we all experience what the noted psychiatrist Hocke describes in his autobiography, *Annual Rings,* when he says that a man cannot understand his own death. "He considers the thought unbearable that this whole world of love and friendship, the world of his work and devotion, should simply be wiped away; unbearable to fall along the side of the road while the others keep going, chatting, as though nothing had happened. That insults all logic," says this physician. And whenever I stand at the death bed or at the grave of a real Christian who died young and not yet finished with life I feel it: there is a person at peace with God, "in God's hands"; and now he is taken away "like a beast of the field." Ought death to be? Ought this boundary, this abyss still exist, when one is in the hands of God, in the hands of the living God? That is, so to speak, the protest that always rings out within us when we have some intimation of that life for which humanity is *properly* destined.

The poet Hölderlin is correct when he says, "May God forgive me, but I cannot fit death into His world." We can only understand the mystery of death if we take seriously the human rebellion against God, so that we see our mortal fate as the "wages of sin."

That is why the barrier of death has been erected. It teaches us that we human beings belong this side of the boundary of mortality; we belong to the dust and stand under judgment. For basically every one of us wants to be God. Nietzsche, as usual, put it very dramatically and impudently when he said, "If there were a God, how could I bear not to be God?" That's the way we are. And therefore the cherubim stand with flashing sword before the eternity of God, "This far and no farther!" That is death as judgment, as end. This is the way it is understood by the account of the Fall in Genesis (3:22).

What Does It Mean to Conquer Death?

The open tomb of Easter is none other than the key point of breakthrough, where the Prince of Life breeched the enemy's front line. Death could not hold him in its armor-plated vault; he burst it open. And the mighty Easter jubilation springs from the fact that *we* too cannot be left in the prison of death. "Can a head leave a member behind, without drawing it after also?" Could grim death be stronger than the Hand by which we are protected? Could it be stronger than the bond of faithfulness that binds the Master and his disciple? In spite of all, could it make us orphans? We would be the most miserable of all humanity. Thank heaven we are not miserable, but are the disciples, the brothers and sisters, of the Risen One. We are his "friends" (Paul Gerhardt) whom he carries safely through hell and death.

Granted, one thing remains. At some time in the future we too must die. No one is spared it, not even we Christians. Jesus too really died. But now there is something decidedly different. This death can no longer get the better of us. It is, indeed, still a serpent, says Luther, but a serpent whose fangs have been pulled. The serpent is still there, and it is still frightening. It is agonizing to live a life whose horizon is still encircled by the scaly coils of the serpent of death. The new situation for us Christians, however, is that this serpent which surrounds our life is *dead*. For those who realize this, it has lost its terror. The biological death which we must die is powerless and is itself dead.

We must tell ourselves very practically that this death is really dead itself. It may no longer tear us from the hand of God; it may no longer lie to us: "Let us eat and drink, for tomorrow we die." It may no longer lie to us about an eternal night of death with its dark thoughts and its even darker realities or even its yawning nothingness.

As the seaman Gorch Fock wrote to his relatives, "If you should hear that our cruiser has been sunk and there are no survivors, don't cry. The sea in which my body sinks is only a puddle in the hollow of my Savior's hand. Nothing can snatch me from that hand." As Gorch Fock wrote that, he certainly realized that the sea can be a frightful maw, and the hands of the torturers into which one can fall are the hands of sadists. But I can get through it all as through a paper-thin wall; for I know who stands with outstretched arms beyond the wall, in whose hands this devouring ocean is just a puddle—a *little* puddle.

How else could there have been anything like the singing death of the martyrs or the first Christians' songs of praise in the face of the lions' open jaws? They were able to sing in spite of everything because their eyes produced a brief double exposure, similar to a film, so that right behind the thin wall of terror they saw the One who received them—no, who stepped right into the middle of things and once more let himself be crucified with them and eaten by the lions. That is the decisive thing. We must really die, but he goes with us, whether in the arena, on the scaffold, or in the hospital. He is beside us.

Thus I close with a gospel word from the great comforter Matthias Claudius and a parting greeting from Hermann Friedrich Kohlbrügge:

> Whoever will not believe in Christ must see how he can get along without Him. You and I can't do that. We need someone to lift and keep us while we live, and to hold our head in His hands when we must die. He can do that superbly, according to what has been written about Him, and we know of no one whom we would rather have. Therefore, when I die—although I no longer die—and someone finds my skull, that skull will preach to him, "I have no eyes, nevertheless I see Him; I have neither brain nor understanding, nevertheless I comprehend Him; I have no lips, nevertheless I kiss Him; I have no tongue, nevertheless I sing His praise with all of you who call upon his name. I am a hard skull, nevertheless I have been wholly softened and melted by His love; I lie out here in the cemetery, nevertheless I am in paradise. All suffering is forgotten. That is what His great love did in us when He bore His cross for us to Golgotha."

16 *Time and Eternity*

Just before midnight on New Year's Eve we will not take our eyes off the clock. But this gaze is different from the way we just glance at a wristwatch to ascertain whether we still have time to get to a meeting or whether the subway train has already left. At this time, at the end of the old year, we have a peculiar and hard-to-define feeling. At other times we use the clock to regulate our movements, so that we arrive here or there on time. On New Year's Eve, however, we don't move at all; we sit among a circle of friends or even alone in some room. It is the time that suddenly moves past us. They are the last minutes of the old year. For a moment we hear how the time, otherwise so still running, begins to roar as it crashes over the spillway of this peculiar midnight. One must surely be rather snobbish or a little insensitive not to feel a bit of a shiver down the back. Why is it that on this night we experience time so differently from other occasions?

Changing Hours, Changing Year

I would like to propose a strange reason: The cause of our experiencing time so differently in this midnight hour from other times lies in the round shape of our clocks (which are still in the majority despite the new digital models). Naturally, I must give some explanation of this assertion.

Since our clocks are round, their hands go in a circle and continually return to their starting point, creating in us the illusion that everything in life repeats itself and that we always can begin again. What I don't get done by six o'clock today I will certainly have behind me by six tomorrow. The hands will circle back to the same position tomorrow that they have today.

In the last night of the year, however, we encounter time differently. Then, for once, it no longer moves in a circle, but linearly. There is no round clock for the year that, after 365 days, begins anew at the figure "twelve." We would have to imagine a very different sort of device to measure the year. It would be a straight line on which every year we live through would be marked off as a tiny segment. And we would creep along this time-line through our whole life. One by one we leave the segments behind us. The hands, in this case, never complete the circle. We can never annul decisions once we have made them.

In that bygone segment of time perhaps we have taken up a profession, we have married or have divorced, we have entered a friendship or have done wrong to someone. All that has now become part of our destiny. Maybe we would do it differently, if we had it to do over again. Yet "what's done is done." Now we must drag along the "baggage of our past" (Anouilh).

The time-line of which I spoke resembles a long corridor with many doors. Year after year we open a new one. But they have no knob on the other side. We can't go back and begin over as the hands on the clock do. And one day—we know not when or where—the corridor comes to an end, irrevocably. The circular paths on our clock faces, however, never end. They therefore lull us into the illusion that things will always go on this way. In that respect the old hourglasses were a better symbol.

On New Year's Eve we discover that in fact things do *not* continue indefinitely, but that every moment of our life is unique and never returns. Our time runs along and one day will also run out. We discover that we are finite.

Our Knowledge About the End

We carry this knowledge of the end around with us all the time, even when we are not aware of it. Without knowing it, we continually think about death. I say something without giving it much thought: "I've got to hurry" or "I have no time," or "You're only young once; I must strike while the iron is hot." And yet in this way I express the fact that I will not live forever. I therefore must parcel out the limited time. I can do no more than use it; I can't stretch it out. "Life is a fleeting shadow," says Shakespeare.

When this fact dawns on us, we experience something of a shock. Maybe some people will consider me a wet blanket if I, in all seriousness, pose the question whether much of our New Year's gaiety and our use of alcohol to dull our senses could be attributed to our desire to drown out the suddenly audible sound of time running out at the end of the year. We go to some pains to wipe these indications of our finitude out of sight. There is, in fact, a sort of game that tries to repress a deep worry or an unbearable problem in our life. Each of us has had the experience of being depressed or totally in despair and then telling ourselves, "I've got to force myself to laugh, no matter what the price." So we go to see a movie that is advertised as sidesplittingly funny. And we indeed slapped our thighs in laughter at some of the comic scenes. But in the background, never completely forgotten, lurked the sorrow and the unsolved problem. And no sooner were the lights back on than the problems returned—unchanged. True joy arises only if I am in harmony from the inside out with myself and with the meaning of my life. Only then have I no more need to repress anything.

I therefore understand very well why people attend a worship service on the last night of the year; they want to hear a word about eternity, and they are moved to pray. It would be stupid to believe that these people are pessimists who mope around, while the people with the firecrackers and the champagne corks are affirming life. The people who urge it to our attention are also seeking joy, only they seek it in other directions, or at least not *only* through fireworks and similar carousing. They know that our finitude is no longer anxiety-producing if we are sheltered by the Lord of time, if we are at peace with him. What lies behind me and what I have done wrong may no longer separate me from him; he makes it right. What lies ahead of me—the new 365 days—I accept from his hand. And nothing will be allowed to touch me which has not passed his scrutiny so that it will serve my best interests.

And when I reach the last stop on the road, he will be waiting for me.

From this harmony with the Lord of time comes a joy that is free of inner repression. The end of the year should be like a red traffic light for us: it should make us stop for a moment, pause, and then pose the question of where we are going.

PART II

The Answer of the Church Year Festivals

1 *Christmas*

Unusual People at the Manger

When Christmas comes around, almost every year a little photo stands on the bookshelf facing my desk. The photo is particularly dear to me. I have it so arranged that my eye falls on it from time to time as I work. It doesn't have a bit of value as a work of art. Somebody or other has simply clipped out the picture of a Christmas play. Even the composition of this scene shows no evidence of what one would call great theater. One sees a large group of mostly younger men in long white robes with candles in their hands walking toward an altar. At this altar, quite obviously a product of the early Victorian period and therefore not at all edifying from an aesthetic point of view, stand, kneel, and lie four men who regard the approaching group with the utmost fright. One holds his hands in front of his eyes, as though he were blinded, another appears to be heading for cover, and a third makes a gesture of surrender. The intention is clear: the white-robed figures are the heavenly choir of angels, and the four men at the altar are the amazed and frightened shepherds.

Often one of my friends, on a visit, reaches for the picture and asks with a little surprise, "Why do you have that standing here?" Usually he looks a bit helpless when he asks, because tact forbids him to add, "and especially such a mediocre picture—a picture without any artistic sense!"

When that happens I like to let my visitors guess a little, so I ask them, "Well, what do you think; who are these people in the picture?" It is really peculiar how almost everyone gives the same answer. They say, "Well, who could it really be? One is inevitably struck by the total, the downright gripping expression on the faces of the performers. They are obviously totally 'involved,' and the drama is certainly much more for them than mere play. Apparently these are people from a Christian congregation, perhaps a select group from the congregation. One could go so far as to suggest that it might possibly be a Bible college or something of the kind."

When that happens I can hardly wait to end the guessing game and let the cat out of the bag. "You have completely missed the mark," I tell them. "But I understand how you came to your conclusion. The people are indeed caught up in the Christmas miracle; they have taken it to heart. They are not at all *acting* their devotion; they are really into it. But it is no Christian men's group, and it's not a Bible college either. It is a photograph of the Christmas celebration at the B____ Prison. Some years ago I spoke there and visited the prisoners in their cells. They listened—well, I can only say like starving men. Later the prison chaplain sent me this picture. Since then I can't part with it. 'You see this young man?' the chaplain said, 'He killed his friend in a fight over a wristwatch. Year after year he is given the same part. He kneels before the manger and says, "I lay in fetters groaning, You came to set me free. . . ." I tell you, when you hear that coming from him, it really gets to you.'"

Why has this picture captivated me so completely, and why does it affect my visitors in the same way? I ask myself in searching self-criticism whether a certain weakness for sentimentality and *kitsch* makes itself apparent in what impresses me. The flicker of the Christmas candles and the gentle festival of love in contrast to murderers and criminals who are here posing as angels—such melodrama is closer to Alfred Hitchcock than to Luke the Evangelist. But I was afraid lest this snobbish interpretation would cut me off from something that touched me at a far deeper level of my being—something that went straight to my heart (and not simply to my nervous system!). A miracle has been caught by the photograph.

The miracle recorded in this picture is that persons come to the manger out of a very shady past and the Christmas light strikes their messed-up lives. By thus striking them, however, it brightens them up. For although they come from bolted cells and will later return to lock and key, now they may stand beneath an open, "unlocked" heaven. Some among them told me that they, like the prodigal son who did an about-face in the pigsty, have learned to believe in this light of blessing and have become new men because of it. They are no longer acting; they are serious about it. They are not reciting verses learned by rote; they are confessing them. And when one of them says, "I lay in fetters groaning, You came to set me free"—that *is* a miracle.

Perhaps one or two of my readers is thinking, "He's really asking too much. Of course criminals should have pastoral care, and, as far as I'm concerned, Christmas celebrations too. But to put me, an upstanding citizen, on the same level with them is pushing Christian charity too far."

It would indeed be wrong and also out of harmony with the Christmas gospel to say that all the differences between gifted and handicapped, successes and failures, righteous and rascals are evened out. The point is entirely different, and I will try to state it in two different ways.

One of the central thoughts is that, at Christmas, God comes to us in the depths. I do not need first to have religious feelings, out of which I then produce some internal and external results, before he comes to me. He comes in the stable, to the disconsolate, the sick, and the despairing; he trudges in the long lines of refugees; and if everyone and everything should desert me in my final hour, I can say, "If I should have to depart, depart not from me." Then he comes even to the dark valley of death. Crib and cross are of the same wood.

And now the *second:* At some time or other in our life, everyone of us is poor. Perhaps it's not visible from the outside, for we human beings know very little about one another. Perhaps I am worried or have been burdened with guilt, or am sick or am goaded by consuming desires that are never fulfilled. The prisoners in the picture represent this side of me. In my case it is kept dark, but in theirs it has broken through. Out of this dark no light could be brought; there is nothing but shadows, labyrinths, and dead ends with no way out. But now the reflection of *another* light shines on their foreheads. Long before they began to ask whether meaning and hope were still possible for them, someone was already on the way. Christmas tells us that God comes for us, no matter where we are. And when everything seems to be finished, that is when God's possibilities begin.

Therefore Christmas will be understood first by those who have no more human hope. One need only read the advice to the lovelorn columns in the papers to learn how numerous they are. Even when they feel God has deserted them, when he seems pushed aside by a gaping nothingness, they can still, with one last thought, grasp the fact that someone is here who wants to be on their side and who does not disdain being identified with them.

In James Baldwin's novel *Another Country* that view is expressed in a worldly—almost too worldly—way, and even more in a style that is definitely not customary in Christian discourse. The young black, Rufus, looks back on a fouled-up life of mistakes and misery. Everything that he believed as a child and that had once wrapped him in paternal security has long ago disappeared or become unreal. Now he stands on a bridge in New York in icy weather, on the verge of jumping to his death. He looks up to heaven (although it doesn't exist for him) and, in wild despair, a curse pours out of him on everything that once provided safety but now is lost. In one breath he swears at God and asks, "Ain't I your baby, too?" And then as he jumps and feels the air whistling around him he repeats his curse, but adds, "I'm coming to you."

Our flesh may well creep when we hear such monstrosities, but then we should pose the question, "Could he have thus cursed God and himself, at the same time addressing God so personally and announcing his arrival, if he had not been touched by the mystery of Christmas?", that mystery that lets him know, "I am mired in the muck of my bungled life. Heaven has no meaning for me any more. But there is Someone who did not stay in heaven but came to me in this muck. Therefore he will pick up, through my crazy ranting, the voice of a homesick child. Even if there is no human being around to hear, he'll be there to receive me."

Perhaps it takes that kind of alienation from the Christmas festivities in order to sort out the real substance they contain from all the mushy sentimentalism and frosting. For the meaning of Christmas is not in befogging the mind, but in comforting the heart that knows it is lost.

Why I Celebrate Christmas

Although Christmas is generally considered to be a festival of light and is celebrated with lots of candles, it sometimes occurs to me that it is now only a shadow for us—the shadow of a Figure who passed by long ago.

Granted, greatness still clings even to the shadow that is cast back towards us. It continues to outline a reality which even the "modern world" with its pride in being practical and unsentimental calls love—albeit with some embarrassment. At Christmas people are nice to each other and enjoy themselves. The antagonisms that really bother them are fended off for the moment and the good-natured law of "don't rock the boat" rules over all. It may sound ironic, but I say it just the same: greatness still clings even to this shadow of things past.

The irony, or rather the sadness that takes refuge in irony, appears when we measure the shadow against the original. What kind of love is it, after all, that does not stem from direct contact with the beloved, but only stays alive in us as a sort of memory and mere echo?

When I am asked why I, as a Christian, celebrate Christmas, I answer first and foremost, "Because here something happens *to* me, therefore something can happen *in* me—but only if I pause and surrender to it."

I live in the name of the miracle that God is no silent universal principle but that he comes to me in the depths. I see that in the One who lies as a child in the manger and is like all the rest of us in every other way. I see there how he whom "heaven and earth could not contain" enters the world of little things—my little things. The world of homelessness and refugee routes; the world of lepers, mental cases, prodigal sons, and poor widows; the world of cheating, dying, and killing.

Once in the history of the world—and it *did* happen once—the incredible occurred and someone stepped forward with the claim that he was God's Son and the assertion that "the Father and I are one" (John 10:30), not proving this claim by supernatural behavior, by astounding people with his wisdom or by imparting knowledge of higher realms, but seeking verification in the depths to which he was willing to descend. A Son of God who defends his title by arguing that he is still brother to the poorest and the guilt-laden, whose burden he takes upon himself! A record like that evokes wondering disbelief—or worship. There is no third alternative. I must worship. That's why I celebrate Christmas.

Of what use is the conventional religious froth that has gathered around this festival? What real good is accomplished by all the pious sentimentalities? Aren't they actually "opium"? Or what difference does it make to me if I see God as simply the creator of galaxies and solar systems or of the microcosm of the atom? What is this God of the greatest and the smallest to me when I feel my conscience bothering me, or loneliness closing in on me, or daily worries clutching at my throat? What do I get out of someone saying to me, "There is a Supreme Intelligence that conceived the created order, invented the laws of causation, and maneuvered the planets into their orbits." I can only respond, "You don't say! A quite fantastic idea, but almost too good to be true!" And then I pick up my paper, or turn on the television, for that would not have been a message that could give me life.

But if someone says to me, "There is One who knows about you, who is concerned when you go your own way, and he has paid a price (specifically, the whole expenditure from crib to cross!) in order to be the star you may look to, the staff you may lean upon, and the spring where you may rest"—if someone tells me *that*, then I sit up and take notice. Because if it is true (if it is really true!) that there is One who is interested in me and who shares my destiny, then, at a single stroke, everything that I previously hoped and feared can be transformed. It could mean a revolution in my life—and in my understanding, too, for that matter.

I think that all atheists, nihilists, and agnostics are correct in one respect (which we have already discussed), namely, when they say that a look at the course of history provides us with no clue for discerning God and "higher thoughts" according to which our world is governed. Christmas, however, teaches us to see our relationship to the world from a completely different point of view. We no longer argue from an orderly universe to God, but we reason from the Child in the manger to the mystery of the world—that world that now holds the manger. For with this Child in the picture, the world centers on him.

I see in this Child, then, the fatherly background to the world. I see that love rules over and in the world, even when I don't understand that rule. If the disclosure of love overwhelms me at *one* point—where Jesus Christ walked the earth and lived upon it—then I can be confident that it is also present where I can no longer understand the course of events.

I would like to illustrate this further by an analogy. When I observe a fine fabric through a magnifying glass, the center of the field is quite clear. At the edges, though, the image begins to blur. However, I do not allow that fact to mislead me into thinking that the fabric itself is fuzzy there. The same thing is true with the marvelous insight which Christmas provides me. Looking at the world through the medium of the Good News, I see the central point with clarity. I see the miracle of love that projects itself into the depths. On the edges, however, beyond the light of Christmas, confusion and distortion reign.

Therefore the eye that wanders afield must reorient itself and look towards the center. It is most remarkable that here the mystery of life is not illuminated by a formula, but by another mystery: by news which is only to be believed and at the same time which can hardly be believed—that God has become human and that now when I am in the dark I am no longer alone. That's why I celebrate Christmas.

2 *Good Friday*

The Greatest Love

One certainly cannot imagine that the image of the noble sufferer, fascinating though it is, could suffice to understand the first word of Jesus from the cross: "Father, forgive them, for they know not what they do" (Luke 23:34). One could certainly not imagine that this statement had anything to do with tolerance or with stoic resignation. In a crowd gone wild, carried away by the power of some demagogue to reckless derision of a serious individual or a respectable institution, it might not be so difficult to say with a certain detachment, "They know not what they do!" In fact a certain feeling of self-satisfaction can come into play at this point, saying to itself, "I am an independent thinker and not simply part of a mob."

On Golgotha, however, this word was spoken by someone whose life was being wrung out of him by the grim charade of the cross. He was in senseless pain, nearly dead of thirst, victim of an execution which did not proceed with the impartiality of a modern judicial process. It was a sadistic orgy, with the jeers and insults of his tormentors pouring on him from all sides. Other powers must surely be at work here to produce that kind word of forgiveness. What powers were they?

Basically, Jesus had *always* practiced what he spoke about in this word from the cross. No one stood up against sin and evil as he did. How he exposed and reprimanded the Pharisees for their hypocrisy! How he drove out the sharp-dealing violators of the temple! With what earnestness he forced tax collectors, adulterers, and even self-satisfied pious people to face their sins! But as much as he hated the sins and the demonic, he likewise loved and sought out people on whom those evil powers had fallen, people who lived in their dark bondage. Therefore, when he said that we should love our neighbor as ourselves, and when he began practicing this love himself and first loved us, he did not mean that we should force ourselves to something like a "feeling of love." We just can't do that, and if we try to anyway, we'll end up, as I mentioned before, tied up in knots. We just *can't* love on demand. So Jesus must have meant something else. And indeed he did.

When Jesus loved guilt-ridden persons and helped them, he saw in them straying children of God. He saw in them human beings whom his Father loved and whose straying caused him sadness. At the same time he saw them as God had originally intended them to be, and therefore he saw through the layers of dirt to the genuine article beneath. Jesus did not *identify* human beings with their guilt; he saw that guilt as foreign, as not really belonging to them, but as binding and mastering them. He wanted to free them again, to take them away from the powers and make them his own. Jesus could love people because he loved through the layers of dirt, so to speak.

I once heard of a pastor to whom a woman complained bitterly about her violent, brutal husband. She confessed openly that she really hated him and that on no account could she love him anymore. The pastor told her that, on such occasions of inner need, she might imagine him as he was during their engagement, how he courted her, how his best side then came to the fore. For *that* was his real personality. The brutality and lack of understanding which gradually came out was to be considered something foreign which had seized upon him and distorted his nature. To the degree that the woman was successful in lovingly pressing through the foreign and seeing the *genuine* in her disfigured husband—to discern the original, so to speak—she could love him again and thereby bring a creative new and constructive initiation into the ruined relationship.

Exactly the same thing happens here with the love and forgiveness of the dying Lord. He pierces through the foreign and disfiguring spirit of sadism, hate, and delusion, seeing all the people who rage around the cross as children of his heavenly Father who have become homeless and miserable. *Those* are the ones he sorrows for; *those* are the ones he loves.

When Jesus speaks these words, "Father, forgive them, for they know not what they do," understood in the above sense, then he is not achieving some miracle of self-control. The accomplishment has nothing at all to do with will power. It is the miracle of an entirely new and God-given way of seeing. The person gifted with this vision that penetrates the layers of dirt, who can still see in the distortion the child of God, will also be able to love.

This change in the manner of seeing is promised to us Christians in an entirely new way. When people do something bad to us and become indebted to us, we must—and we may—tell ourselves, "Jesus Christ died for this husband who deceived me, for this wife who vents her inexplicable hatred on me, for these people who cheated me. They are the ones for whom he paid a high price; they are the ones he has embraced with his love." Those who can then step beneath the cross and let themselves be given *this* vision in the midst of often turbulent controversies with other people, those who are able to see others as, in a mysterious way, children of God, will stop being a mere echo of such controversies and will stop simply reacting to them. Instead, the creative impulse of love will come into their life.

In other words, we must begin to love. Then so much will change that it will bring tears to our eyes. That is why the moment when this word was spoken from the cross is so tremendous. Here was someone who could love his enemies and his attackers because he *saw* them in a totally new way. Since that moment a new possibility of seeing has emerged in the world. It is intended for every one of us.

Being Forsaken by God

According to the earliest account, the last word which Jesus spoke as he died was more a cry than a word, "My God, my God, why hast thou forsaken me?" (Mark 15:34). Isn't this parting cry the confession of defeat? The sun quit shining. It could no longer look upon the atrocity. He cried out—but God was silent. Once again: wasn't that defeat?

Yet in this death there is something else—something full of mystery. What was going on, then, in that horrible outcry of one who apparently had been forsaken by God? Is he just shouting about his misery and his despair to the crowd that has collected around his cross? Is this outcry a sort of unburdening of his soul? No, it is something entirely different.

First, it is by no means just a random outcry, but a strictly liturgical prayer (Ps. 22:1). The crucified one is praying a psalm. He therefore utters a word of God in order to lament being forsaken by God. Thus, despite his need, he remains connected to the divine power circuit. Here below he grasps a word of the eternal God and reaches back up to him with it.

Those who thus express their fear and need by making the word of God himself their witness no longer wander and grope their way through cosmic darkness and a forsaken no man's land. They pray among the people of God; they have patriarchs and prophets beside them, all of whom listened to that word and then sent it worshipfully back to heaven.

And there is one more thing. In that God-forsaken shout, Jesus did not address the *people* in order to summon them as witnesses to his agony. Nor did he call out his need into the empty, black night of Golgotha. He had *Another* to whom he turned. He spoke to God himself about his forsakenness. He did not repudiate God by blasphemously passing judgment on the divine majesty and by crying out his denunciation of God's failure to act; he shouts, "*My* God, *my* God." And therefore he still *had* him; the forsakenness has already been conquered in the cry; he has left it behind. The only one who is really forsaken by God is the dullard who cannot find words any more, who knows no addressee, and who is so far gone in his denial of God that he *cannot* even denounce, or hate, or repudiate him. For how could you denounce someone, how could you hate someone and repudiate him, if he didn't even exist? Jesus, however, confessed his mortal forsakenness to the father. By confessing it to *him,* he *is* no longer forsaken. Now someone is there to whom he can tell it, and who is still his God.

Then, in this call out of the utmost depths and the deepest darkness, the whole mystery of the Son of God manifests itself. On the one hand he tastes the bitterest woes of human life and, as a companion to his fellow humans, walks through vales of tears and wildernesses whose depths exceed those experienced by anyone else. From that time on, whoever suffers can tell himself, "The Crucified has suffered worse." Whoever is lonely may realize that the Crucified has walked through stretches of alienation from humanity and from God that none of us has had to endure.

That is one side of it. He has, by crying out his forsakenness by God, become completely human. He has become the most deeply bowed human, stricken most horribly by suffering and death. And at the same time he is the Son of God who, when the darkness seeks to grasp him, himself grasps the hand of the Father by calling upon him.

Thus, although he is most horribly abandoned, he is nevertheless sheltered in those hands and removed from all misery. By being drawn into nothingness, he is held by the divine majesty itself. By being lifted up on a cross, he is secretly lifted onto an invisible throne. By crying out as the groaning creation, he lives in eternal dialogue with the Father. He is man and he is God; he is bowed down into death and raised into life.

That is what religious people have meant to express when they see in the raising of the cross, and therefore in the apparent triumph of death, a mysterious intimation of that other raising that was proclaimed on the third day. That is what the Romanesque artists intended when they placed a crown on the Crucified. As in a double exposure, one must see the crown of thorns and the kingly crown, shame and fame, death and eternity, humanity and divinity superimposed. Only then can one believe the mystery of Jesus.

3 *Easter*

Easter Questions Us

Remarkable! Whenever I spoke about death and eternal life, the people came in especially large crowds. Young people were and are in the majority. What are they looking for from this subject? Were they bored with life? Was it a flight into the beyond? Were they seeking the "opium of the people" that would numb them to the boredom and emptiness of everyday life?

I interpret this throng of people differently. Many conversations and letters have put me on the right track. We are concerned here with a question that plagues everyone who ever takes a minute to stop and think.

Is the "drama" of my life to be nothing more than getting up, working, television in the evening, and going to bed, following one another in an endless chain until one day when the candle is blown out? Would this festival of candles have been worth it? Had life been worth the effort at all?

And yet another question will not leave me alone: I want to make something out of my life. It should be successful. I realize my "responsibility." But who is it, anyway, who asks me so that I must "respond." Is it merely a dialogue with my conscience? Or will there one day come a moment of truth, when I must stand up and give an accounting? Is there an eternity in which my life does not simply "go out," but where I am awaited?

These questions bring us to the subject of Easter.

A few years ago one of my dearest students died. During the last night I was with him and held his hand. At six in the morning the little bell in a nearby chapel rang. The dying man brightened up, "Do you hear the Easter bells? (It was in the fall and by no means Easter time.) Now he is coming to fetch me. I see beyond death. I see the other bank."

What happened to turn the miserable working-day bell into the pealing of Easter chimes for him? It was not the belief in an "immortality of the soul" that permitted him to brave death. It was something different. He knew that Jesus had accepted him and that this Lord of his was the Prince of Easter. As he heard the little bell, something became overwhelmingly clear to him: This Jesus who has tasted a much more bitter death than I beckons to me from eternity. He has placed his hand upon me, so he will not leave me in the hands of death.

That is the victorious certainty of Easter. The mystery of our life ultimately boils down to one single question: Whom do I trust—the claws of a fate that crushes me, or that hand that gives me shelter and that will not let me go—even on the other bank?

At the bed of a dying person Christians are accustomed to pray the words of a hymn which contains everything that we need to know. Read this verse from the hymn "O Sacred Head, Now Wounded" through slowly and absorb what it says:

> Lord, be my consolation;
> Shield me when I must die;
> Remind me of thy Passion
> When my last hour draws nigh.
> These eyes, new faith receiving,
> From thee shall never move;
> For he who dies believing
> Dies safely in thy love.

Life from the Resurrection

There is nothing in life so certain as the fact that we must die. If the Easter message is to help us cope with death, then it must be at least equally certain. But is it not grotesque to assume that we can be helped by an ancient chronicle's strange story that the grave of Jesus of Nazareth was empty on the third day and therefore we too will rise from death and decay? Can it deal successfully with the basic fact of our biological end? The words of the psalm about people dying "like the beasts that perish" (Ps. 49:12,20) sound somewhat drastic, but they are still true, and our experience confirms them. But to say that Christ brings us as his "friends" through the night of death into an eternal life—what experience could confirm *that?* Would anyone seriously doubt the certainty of the Pythagorean theorem if someone told of a dream in which he had seen totally different geometrical relationships? Could we (and this would be a similar question) doubt the certainty and finality of death if we read in old records that some people in a long ago province had a vision that their spiritual leader had come back to life?

We must honestly concede that it is unbearable for all of us, Christians included, if our destiny in time and eternity depends on a matter so relative and shaky as a thousand-year-old record, with all its attendant historical problems. An absolute such as faith in Easter's victory over death ought not hang by the thin thread of such vague relativities.

The Easter story, however, tells us that that is not the case. It is interesting to note how Jesus Christ himself treats the question of resurrection in the parable of the rich man and poor Lazarus (Luke 16:19ff.). There sits the rich man in the hell of eternal separation from God, thinking about his frivolous five brothers who still heedlessly enjoy the light of day. He tries to figure out how they could be given such a healthy shock that they would steer clear of the same catastrophe that had pulled him into the abyss. Then he hits upon an idea. Why not ask Abraham to send a messenger from the beyond to the brothers? An eyewitness account of heaven and hell, eternal life and eternal death, should be an impressive warning! Abraham, however, decisively vetoes the idea. He lets the rich man know that his brothers have "Moses and the prophets"; they could discover everything necessary from the Word of God without such doings from the beyond. If they wanted to barricade themselves against this word, then it wouldn't make any impression on them either if someone came from the dead and entertained them with eyewitness accounts. Abraham meant that, if someone is not inwardly touched by the reality around him, and if he won't tolerate any interruptions while "sowing his wild oats," then he will certainly find sufficient reasons for dismissing such miracles from the beyond. Perhaps he would talk about "spiritualistic delusions."

One could say exactly the same thing about the disciples on Easter morning. They just couldn't have brought themselves to believe that the dead Jesus had supposedly risen from the tomb, if they had not believed his *word*. There were plenty of other explanations available, such as the well-known ones about the body of Jesus being stolen or being carried off by some of his followers in order to generate a clever legend. So far, a miracle has never brought anyone to faith. There is always another way to explain it. (That is why Jesus acted so cautiously when he was supposed to legitimate his ministry through miracles.)

For that reason the empty tomb didn't bring the disciples to faith either. Instead something quite different happened. Faced with the empty tomb, it was as though scales suddenly fell from their eyes and they subsequently recognized how many dotted lines in the life of the Savior converged on this one point where the event of Easter broke in upon them. What they experienced on that morning was merely the last phase of a sequence of events of which they had been eyewitnesses, although, to be sure, they had completely missed the point at the time. Now it was clear to them—in retrospect.

When someone says, "Your sins are forgiven" and when

the person so addressed really gets up and goes away a new man, then the speaker could only be someone who was not entangled in the sinful web of everything human; in some mysterious way he must stand outside it. When someone says, "Young man, I say to you, arise!" and when the dead man really rises and is given back to his mourning mother, that event could only happen through a person before whom death must retreat as a "last enemy." And again: the passage "come unto me all who are weary and heavy laden" could only be spoken by someone who, although he understands all weariness and affliction and shares it like a brother, nevertheless draws his life from other sources and gives his love from which streams of living water flow.

The disciples, indeed, had experienced all of that, but because of their amazingly limited vision, they had not caught on until it suddenly dawned on them in the light of Easter. The whole earthly life of the Lord who went about the countryside healing, helping, forgiving, and providing new beginnings all at once became transparent for them. The mute, empty senselessness of Golgotha had previously thrown them into a panic and left them in despair; now those events became eloquent and persuasive witnesses to them. They suddenly realized that while he had walked the earth and shared their daily life, they had not understood him at all. Of course their hearts had burned within them and they felt as though they were in the shadow of a tremendous figure (Luke 24:32), but only now came the discovery of *who* it was who had walked with them. Gradually the light illuminated his enigmatic words and deeds. The heavens opened above him whom they had considered one of themselves, albeit the greatest; yet he was the "totally other," who came from the eternity of the Father to share their everyday earthly life for a little while.

Therefore the fact of Easter will never convince us if the Man does not. The empty tomb will not force us to believe, and no account of the resurrection will do it, only this resurrected Figure himself can. In the encounter with Jesus of Nazareth we perceive that we have found someone who, out of love, bound his fate up with our own and remained true to us. Only on that basis can we sing the Chorale from the "St. Matthew Passion": "When I one day depart, Depart thou not from me."

Once gripped by this solidarity with Jesus Christ I know that he will not permit death to step between himself and me, but that I will be protected by him through all eternity.

In that case, perhaps our experience is similar to that of the disciples—it only dawns on us later and afterward. Perhaps at first we understand nothing more than that a man appeared on earth who loved unconditionally and without counting the cost. That is certainly true, but it is not the whole story. We would only have touched the hem of his garment; we would not yet have seen his face. Yet it would be a start. For I put no store in the crass alternatives that one must either believe everything at once or else be an unbeliever. In faith too there is growth, small beginnings and eventual fulfillment. One thing however remains sure: if we begin by reading the Gospel as though it were a completely innocuous novel about various mundane matters (and why not?), one day we will discover that this approach doesn't work out—that totally different realities lie undisclosed. Only then do we hit the truth. The windows will light up and the Prince of life will say to us, "You shall not die, but live."

A Pensive Easter Stroll

Early one Easter afternoon my doorbell rang. A young student, with whom I had only a fleeting acquaintance, stood at the door. He apologized politely for disturbing me and asked for a chance to talk. I saw at once that something was bothering him, so I suggested that we take a walk, since the weather was so nice. As we sauntered down towards the water, I didn't even have to ask him about his problem. He brought it up himself.

"Lately I have done a lot of thinking about questions of faith," he said. "It relates to some experiences that were hard for me to take. But that is not so important. At any rate it suddenly occurred to me that I was up against the key question of our life. If we want to go to the movies this evening, we ask, 'What is playing?' I suddenly asked myself, 'What is actually playing in my life? Who is the director, and what is playing the leading role?'"

I: "A very reasonable and obvious question. It's remarkable that most people ask it only about the movies and not about their own lives."

He: "Yes, that suddenly became clear to me. Then last week I heard the 'St. Matthew Passion.' I did not go, as you might think, for religious reasons nor for strictly musical ones. I liked the theme—the life and death of one of the most essentially 'human' beings. Certainly there I would have some light shed on that question of managing one's life. Do you understand?"

I: "And how! Did you get your money's worth?"

He: "It really got to me. Precisely because the 'St. Matthew Passion' is so undogmatic."

I: "What do you mean by 'undogmatic'?"

He: "Well, that it doesn't talk about the resurrection, as they do in church. The great closing chorale simply mourns the passing of this unique and majestic person. It ends with a very human tear—and no resurrection dogma."

Before I could slip in a question he immediately went on: "Something human like that is understandable. Everyone knows the feeling of sadness evoked by the fact that even the greatest of us must die, just as the brightest meteor blazes only for a moment across the sky. I ask you, why are the churches in Germany so full on Good Friday, and why has this crowd shrunk so considerably on Easter? People are gripped by death, because they themselves must die. The resurrection, however, will become clearer to them in nature than in that embarrassing dogma in which the sadness of Good Friday—pardon me—is repudiated in such an unsatisfactory way."

I: "Your analysis would certainly apply to most people. The only question is what conclusion is to be drawn from it. If I understand you correctly, you think that everyone from the creator of the 'St. Matthew Passion' to the smartly dressed people around us can identify with the moving human aspect of the death on Good Friday, but not with the empty tomb on Easter and other miracles of that sort?"

He: "That's exactly what I mean. And you know (he said this very emotionally), it is downright puzzling to me that someone like you, who lectures on Kant and whom I've recently seen at a soccer game, sides with the miracle of the resurrection. Yet that is the case—or is it?"

I: "Absolutely. If Christ did not rise from the dead, then his life and his work are refuted. From Bethlehem to Golgotha there is no scene that is not indirectly illuminated by the light of Easter. Every event is undergirded by the certainty that the course of his life is not limited by death, but that it is stronger than death and reaches beyond it. If I didn't know that, and if I were not likewise convinced that Christ and those who belong to him—including me—also will pass beyond death, then I would hardly dare to pose the question, 'What is playing in my life?'"

He: "I'm really glad that you spoke so bluntly and simply. But you really leave me at a loss. Are the rest of us, then, not Christian, since we prefer Good Friday and find Easter beyond us? Why then is the passion history so detailed in the Gospels, while the Easter accounts are so brief? Why does the 'St. Matthew Passion' conclude with the burial of Jesus, without dealing with the mystery of the Third Day? Isn't it always the *human* fate of the Crucified that moves us, and isn't Easter, by contrast, a doctrinaire, forced, and convoluted addition? The one is packed with life, and the other is an anemic doctrine. Well, I've been very outspoken, but I can't keep still about it. It won't let me."

I: "There's no reason in the world to keep still about it. Faith can't be obtained by dishonesty or repressing doubts. Permit me a quite naive observation. Have you ever read the Easter stories while someone dear to you was dying—your father, your mother, your friend? No? Well, I have. Situations like that are a stern test of authenticity. They detect every false note. And speculation is simply out of the question when you are pushed back to basics. But the Easter stories are themselves basic. They have a freshness that overpowers the melancholy of the grave. You must try that sometime. There's nothing 'anemic' about it."

He: "Good, that's an idea that bears investigation. But it's remarkable that you, trained scientifically, should suggest it, because it's far from scientific."

I: "There are moments when anyone who follows a scientific calling must acknowledge the basis on which he builds his life and the principles which form his thought."

He: "As a theologian, of course, you are well versed in speculating. (Excuse me!) Therefore I appreciate your coming at me from an entirely different angle. But let's get back to Good Friday. Please say a little more about why people are so wrapped up in its humanity and why they are convinced that Easter is such an unpalatable affair."

I: "It is precisely opposite to the way you think it is. For the people of the New Testament and also for Bach, Easter is sure and certain. Their faith draws its life from the mystery of God himself having come among us in the person of Jesus. It was the most self-evident thing in the world to them that in Jesus of Nazareth we are dealing with God. But that he left his heavenly glory, that he shared the burden of guilt, suffering, and death with his human brothers and sisters—*that* was the great mystery. Therefore in their narratives and meditations they applied every effort to that amazing fact—that he really and truly lived and suffered as a human being, as one of us.

"Today, you see, many of us say, 'Good Friday is so human and therefore so believable; Easter, however, is a myth.' Through the centuries the great Christians have thought exactly the opposite: 'Easter is clear. Compared to the Son of God, death is a puny runt. But that this Son of God should have become human like us—perhaps *that* is a myth, or maybe he only seemed human. Possibly his body was not real.' That is the approach they take in struggling with the man Jesus and the human-ness of Good Friday."

He: "That means, then, that people used to struggle with Good Friday, and that today we must struggle with Easter?"

I: "Exactly."

He: "Wait a minute! Excuse me, but that's going to take some time to digest."

4 *Pentecost*

The Miracle of the Spirit

The concept "spirit" in German has a wider range than in English. It can signify the ultimate in rational comprehension or intuitive understanding. People who are considered *"geistvoll"* or "spiritful" usually have the additional gift of sharply formulating ideas. In English the best translation might be "brilliant." The German usages, however, underline the relation of "spirit" to clarity and lucidity.

When it comes to the "Holy" Spirit, though, which we remember especially at Pentecost, aren't things entirely different? Anyone who has heard and seen a pentecostal black congregation in ecstasy would say it was the opposite of a clear and rational spirit; people were carried away with a wild and irrational frenzy. Must anyone who becomes involved with the Holy Spirit expect to go a little crazy? An uninvolved observer might think so. The eye- and ear-witnesses of what happened on the first Pentecost, at any rate, received this impression. (One can look it up in the second chapter of Acts.) They supposed that the disciples, upon whom the Spirit had come, were drunk; they had bent their elbows a little too often—that was all.

As usual, there was more to it than met the eye. Again and again these disciples let themselves be imprisoned, stoned, and persecuted for what they had seen in so-called delirium. That should give us pause. Visions that are merely the product of alcohol usually end up as hangovers. And in no case, once sober again, would a person let his head be chopped off for those visions. You voluntarily offer your head only for something that you consider of the utmost importance when you are completely sober and realistic. It has to be a matter for which, after rigorous calculation, you believe the price of your life is not too high. Whoever rereads that account of Pentecost will discover that the people involved in fact calculated and argued with utmost sobriety. The reports themselves are objective and terse—almost like police records.

But where does that leave us with the curious question of the Holy Spirit?

The disciples are trying to say, "Suddenly it was as though scales had dropped from our eyes. Of course we already knew that Jesus had been crucified and had risen. But we couldn't get a hold on it. It was Greek to us; it wasn't 'relevant' for our lives. But now, all at once we recognize what it means; now it *speaks* to us. Now it hits home to us in such a way that we must live differently."

Let me try to use a simple illustration to clarify what is going on.

We have all, at some time, visited a cathedral with stained glass windows. Often they portray biblical stories: Adam and Eve, the prophets, Mary at the Cross, the women at Jesus' tomb. As long as we just walk around the outside of the building, we see nothing of all this. The windows appear black and monotonous. But as soon as we enter the interior they light up in the fullness of their colors. They "preach" the old stories. Although the panes are the same, they look completely different, depending on whether you are inside or outside.

We note that the same thing is true elsewhere in life. If we look at a mother's love simply from the outside, as a coldly biological observer, so to speak, it likewise appears somewhat dull—just a sort of hormone-controlled monkey love. But if we think about our own mother, about the safety of her protection, the warmth of her heart, and her loving thoughtfulness, then the picture of "mother" immediately blossoms into warm full color. We are then seeing mother love from the "inside," as a child that belongs, or once belonged, to its mother.

It's the same way with the Holy Spirit. He leads us into the interior of events where the windows light up. At that point we cease being mere onlookers, intruders, and "outsiders." It therefore becomes clear to us that the Father addresses *us* and that we are *his* children. We realize that it wasn't just anybody who was nailed to the cross, but that he died for *me*. I am drawn into the events in the windows; now I must join the game. I am present at the cross and the open tomb. Now I know that here *my* guilt is forgiven and a new life is opened to *me*.

That is what the disciples meant when they said that it was like scales falling from their eyes. Suddenly it became clear to each of them: I am the one who is involved here. God has noticed me and my life. I can no longer avoid this gaze. I am asked whether I agree to that or whether I turn my back and go back to my old ways.

Pentecost shows me that the Bible is no archaic document that lies far back in the past, but that it is addressed to me. The Holy Spirit is the spirit of making things real. He accomplishes the miracle of making seers out of the blind.